# Children's Mathematics

Geoffrey B. Saxe, *Editor*
University of California, Los Angeles

Maryl Gearhart, *Editor*
University of California, Los Angeles

---

NEW DIRECTIONS FOR CHILD DEVELOPMENT
WILLIAM DAMON, *Editor-in-Chief*
*Clark University*

Number 41, Fall 1988

Paperback sourcebooks in
The Jossey-Bass Social and Behavioral Sciences Series

Jossey-Bass Inc., Publishers
San Francisco • London

Geoffrey B. Saxe, Maryl Gearhart (eds.).
*Children's Mathematics.*
New Directions for Child Development, no. 41.
San Francisco: Jossey-Bass, 1988.

**New Directions for Child Development**
William Damon, *Editor-in-Chief*

Copyright © 1988 by Jossey-Bass Inc., Publishers
and
Jossey-Bass Limited

Copyright under International, Pan American, and Universal Copyright Conventions. All rights reserved. No part of this issue may be reproduced in any form—except for brief quotation (not to exceed 500 words) in a review or professional work—without permission in writing from the publishers.

*New Directions for Child Development* is published quarterly by Jossey-Bass Inc., Publishers (publication number USPS 494-090). Second-class postage paid at San Francisco, California, and at additional mailing offices. POSTMASTER: Send address changes to Jossey-Bass Inc., Publishers, 350 Sansome Street, San Francisco, California 94104.

**Editorial correspondence** should be sent to the Editor-in-Chief, William Damon, Department of Psychology, Clark University, Worcester, Massachusetts 01610.

Library of Congress Catalog Card Number LC 85-644581

International Standard Serial Number ISSN 0195-2269

International Standard Book Number ISBN 1-55542-884-3

Cover art by WILLI BAUM

Manufactured in the United States of America. Printed on acid-free paper.

# *Ordering Information*

The paperback sourcebooks listed below are published quarterly and can be ordered either by subscription or single copy.

Subscriptions cost $60.00 per year for institutions, agencies, and libraries. Individuals can subscribe at the special rate of $45.00 per year *if payment is by personal check*. (Note that the full rate of $60.00 applies if payment is by institutional check, even if the subscription is designated for an individual.) Standing orders are accepted.

Single copies are available at $14.95 when payment accompanies order. (California, New Jersey, New York, and Washington, D.C., residents please include appropriate sales tax.) For billed orders, cost per copy is $14.95 plus postage and handling.

Substantial discounts are offered to organizations and individuals wishing to purchase bulk quantities of Jossey-Bass sourcebooks. Please inquire.

Please note that these prices are for the academic year 1988–89 and are subject to change without notice. Also, some titles may be out of print and therefore not available for sale.

To ensure correct and prompt delivery, all orders must give either the *name of an individual* or an *official purchase order number*. Please submit your order as follows:

*Subscriptions:* specify series and year subscription is to begin.
*Single Copies:* specify sourcebook code (such as, CD1) and first two words of title.

Mail orders for United States and Possessions, Australia, New Zealand, Canada, Latin America, and Japan to:
  Jossey-Bass Inc., Publishers
  350 Sansome Street
  San Francisco, California 94104

Mail orders for all other parts of the world to:
  Jossey-Bass Limited
  28 Banner Street
  London EC1Y 8QE


*New Directions for Child Development Series*
William Damon, *Editor-in-Chief*

CD1  *Social Cognition,* William Damon
CD2  *Moral Development,* William Damon
CD3  *Early Symbolization,* Howard Gardner, Dennie Wolf

CD4   *Social Interaction and Communication During Infancy,* Ina Č. Užgiris
CD5   *Intellectual Development Beyond Childhood,* Deanna Kuhn
CD6   *Fact, Fiction, and Fantasy in Childhood,* Ellen Winner, Howard Gardner
CD7   *Clinical-Developmental Psychology,* Robert L. Selman, Regina Yando
CD8   *Anthropological Perspectives on Child Development,* Charles M. Super, Sara Harkness
CD9   *Children's Play,* Kenneth H. Rubin
CD10  *Children's Memory,* Marion Perlmutter
CD11  *Developmental Perspectives on Child Maltreatment,* Ross Rizley, Dante Cicchetti
CD12  *Cognitive Development,* Kurt W. Fischer
CD13  *Viewing Children Through Television,* Hope Kelly, Howard Gardner
CD14  *Children's Conceptions of Health, Illness, and Bodily Functions,* Roger Bibace, Mary E. Walsh
CD15  *Children's Conceptions of Spatial Relationships,* Robert Cohen
CD16  *Emotional Development,* Dante Cicchetti, Petra Hesse
CD17  *Developmental Approaches to Giftedness and Creativity,* David Henry Feldman
CD18  *Children's Planning Strategies,* David Forbes, Mark T. Greenberg
CD19  *Children and Divorce,* Lawrence A. Kurdek
CD20  *Child Development and International Development: Research-Policy Interfaces,* Daniel A. Wagner
CD21  *Levels and Transitions in Children's Development,* Kurt W. Fischer
CD22  *Adolescent Development in the Family,* Harold D. Grotevant, Catherine R. Cooper
CD23  *Children's Learning in the "Zone of Proximal Development,"* Barbara Rogoff, James V. Wertsch
CD24  *Children in Families Under Stress,* Anna-Beth Doyle, Dolores Gold, Debbie S. Moscowitz
CD25  *Analyzing Children's Play Dialogues,* Frank Kessel, Artin Göncü
CD26  *Childhood Depression,* Dante Cicchetti, Karen Schneider-Rosen
CD27  *The Development of Reading Skills,* Thomas H. Carr
CD28  *Children and Computers,* Elisa L. Klein
CD29  *Peer Conflict and Psychological Growth,* Marvin W. Berkowitz
CD30  *Identity in Adolescence: Processes and Contents,* Alan S. Waterman
CD31  *Temperament and Social Interaction in Infants and Children,* Jacqueline V. Lerner, Richard M. Lerner
CD32  *Early Experience and the Development of Competence,* William Fowler
CD33  *Children's Intellectual Rights,* David Moshman
CD34  *Maternal Depression and Infant Disturbance,* Edward Z. Tronick, Tiffany Field
CD35  *How Children and Adolescents View the World of Work,* John H. Lewko
CD36  *Symbolic Development in Atypical Children,* Dante Cicchetti, Marjorie Beeghly
CD37  *Adolescent Social Behavior and Health,* Charles E. Irwin, Jr.
CD38  *Children's Gender Schemata,* Lynn S. Liben, Margaret L. Signorella
CD39  *Developmental Psychopathology and Its Treatment,* Ellen D. Nannis, Philip A. Cowan
CD40  *Parental Behavior in Diverse Societies,* Robert A. LeVine, Patrice M. Miller, Mary Maxwell West

# Contents

**Editors' Notes** 1
Geoffrey B. Saxe, Maryl Gearhart

**1. Universals in the Development of Early Arithmetic Cognition** 5
*Alice Klein, Prentice Starkey*
Research on young children's arithmetic knowledge reveals cultural universals as well as cultural variations in the course of arithmetic development.

**2. Mathematics Learning in Japanese, Chinese, and American Classrooms** 27
*James W. Stigler, Michelle Perry*
Differences across cultures in classroom instruction may contribute to superior performance by Asian children on tests of mathematics achievement.

**3. Social and Motivational Bases for Mathematical Understanding** 55
*Giyoo Hatano*
Encountering novel problems continuously, being encouraged to seek comprehension, freedom from urgent need to get rewards, and dialogical interaction all aid mathematical understanding.

**4. Mathematical Concepts in Everyday Life** 71
*Terezinha N. Carraher, Analucia D. Schliemann, David W. Carraher*
Children and adults with limited schooling form complex mathematical understandings in the course of everyday cultural practices.

**5. Hot Mathematics** 89
*Herbert P. Ginsburg, Kirsten A. Asmussen*
The development of mathematical thinking involves more than cognition alone—affect, motivation, and personality are crucial.

**Index** 113

# Editors' Notes

The purpose of this volume is to bring together researchers who share a concern with the interplay between sociocultural and developmental processes in children's mathematics learning. While each of the chapters is a presentation of a different research direction, across chapters there are related issues that motivate the separate endeavors. The issues include the universality of children's mathematics across cultures, sociocultural and affective processes that lead children to form mathematical understandings of different types, and the role of formal educational processes in children's developing mathematical understandings. In addition, four of the five chapters include outlines of recommended educational applications drawn from basic research. The authors are well-known researchers from the United States, Japan, and Brazil, each of whom has made important contributions to understanding mathematical development in children and adults.

In the opening chapter, Klein and Starkey present a three-component model of arithmetical development in very young children. They use this model as a basis to consider developmental processes in early mathematics learning that may be universal across cultural contexts. To support their framework, they bring together a wide range of recent research conducted in both Western and non-Western cultures. The chapter offers both a conceptually elegant account of early arithmetic and, in its emphasis on universals, provides a useful contrast to the subsequent four chapters—chapters in which authors consider links between mathematics learning and particular social contexts of development.

Next, in Chapter Two, Stigler and Perry show that cultures differ in the ways they organize mathematical learning experiences—differences that may lead children to construct different levels and kinds of mathematical competence. In a comparative study of mathematics teaching in elementary school classrooms in Japan, China, and the United States, Stigler and Perry find that U.S. children lag far behind their Japanese and Chinese peers across a wide range of measures of mathematical competence. The authors make a strong case that differences in the classroom organization of mathematics lessons across cultures contribute to differences in children's mathematics ability. They document classroom factors associated with differences in children's competence and offer the notion of "coherence" for the comparative analysis of mathematics curricula and teaching practices, describing ways in which teaching in U.S. classrooms is less coherent than it is in Japanese and Chinese classrooms.

In Chapter Three, Hatano shifts the focus to cultural differences in mathematics in out-of-school contexts and the consequences of these differences for the nature of children's mathematical competence. Hatano presents a model of cognitive and motivational processes in mathematics learning and uses this model to contrast the competence of abacus experts in Japan and street vendors in Brazil. Abacus experts—children who have no difficulty producing very rapid calculations of multidigit numbers on a real or imaginary abacus—acquire their skills in contexts that value speed rather than the logic of computation, whereas street vendors acquire their skills in contexts in which they must make conceptually explicit the logic of their calculations. Hatano shows that abacus experts develop high levels of arithmetical proficiency but little conceptual understanding, whereas street vendors, though slower, have a rich understanding of the logic of their computations. Based on his analysis of the social and motivational conditions that promote conceptual competence in street vendors, Hatano proposes instructional strategies for motivating conceptual understanding in school mathematics learning.

In Chapter Four, Carraher, Schliemann, and Carraher probe further into the nature of mathematical competence in out-of-school cultural practices and point to the ways in which representational systems and social situations are critical analytic constructs in understanding the character of children's mathematical competence. The authors review a number of their studies with Brazilian children and adults engaged in everyday cultural practices from street vending to fishing. A central theme is that people with little or no schooling construct complex mathematical concepts in such practices—concepts that may be rich conceptual constructions but at the same time have limited extension. Carraher and colleagues analyze the ways that everyday practices may promote rich mathematical knowledge and then consider how educators may profitably incorporate features of these practices in the classroom.

In the final chapter, Ginsburg and Asmussen discuss the way affect, belief, and motive are inherently interwoven with children's and adults' developing mathematical understanding, offering a preliminary treatment of "hot mathematics." The authors present a case study approach that reveals the phenomenology of people's experience of mathematical problem solving and the ways affect is infused with individuals' involvement and avoidance of mathematics. The chapter contains compelling arguments for the need for more comprehensive models of cognitive development, ones in which the dynamics of personality are elevated to a more central status in the analysis of cognitive developmental processes. Ginsburg and Asmussen close by pointing to the importance of "hot mathematics" in conceptualizing meaningful learning at school.

Each of these five chapters represents a distinct new direction in research on children's mathematics. It is our hope that, through exposure to the diversity of research questions represented in this volume, readers will gain a respect for the complexity of children's mathematics learning—particularly for the intricate ways that sociocultural and affected processes are interwoven with the developmental process. Gaining appreciation of these processes is critical not only for basic researchers but also for those educators seeking to apply basic research findings to the classroom.

Geoffrey B. Saxe<br>
Maryl Gearhart<br>
Editors

*Geoffrey B. Saxe is associate professor at the Graduate School of Education, University of California, Los Angeles. His research has focused on the interplay between social and developmental processes in children's mathematics.*

*Maryl Gearhart is assistant research educationist at the Graduate School of Education, University of California, Los Angeles. Her research has included studies of mother-child and peer interaction.*

*Children's knowledge of arithmetic emerges prior to formal instruction in school. Some processes and sequences in early arithmetic development extend across cultural boundaries.*

# Universals in the Development of Early Arithmetic Cognition

*Alice Klein, Prentice Starkey*

This chapter examines the emergence and development of arithmetic cognition in young children before they receive formal arithmetic instruction in school. Our central concern is to specify those aspects of early arithmetic development that are universal across sociocultural contexts. The universalist perspective is perhaps unique in a volume on culture and children's mathematical thinking because it emphasizes commonalities rather than differences in the development of arithmetic cognition. We believe, however, that this perspective is essential to the theoretical problem of formulating general principles of arithmetic development. Furthermore, specifying cultural universals in early arithmetic cognition can serve as a backdrop for analyzing cultural variations in arithmetic processes and their influence on the course of arithmetic development within particular cultural contexts.

Our focus on universals in children's developing arithmetic cognition

---

Order of authorship was determined alphabetically. Appreciation is extended to Maryl Gearhart and Geoffrey Saxe, who commented on an earlier draft of this chapter.

is based on the epistemological position that number is a natural domain of human knowledge. As such, it has unique properties that constrain the ontogenesis of numerical concepts in any cultural context. It also follows from this position that the emergence and development of numerical concepts is not dependent on formal instruction. Thus, in order to reveal most clearly the universal aspects of arithmetic development, we examine the period of early childhood during which specific cultural experiences such as schooling play a less important role in the development of children's arithmetic thinking.

The assumption that children begin to develop knowledge about arithmetic prior to formal instruction in school can be found in the developmental theories of both Piaget ([1941] 1952) and Vygotsky (1978). Over the past decade, a considerable body of evidence has been amassed to support this assumption (for example, Gelman and Gallistel, 1978; Ginsburg and Russell, 1981; Saxe, Guberman, and Gearhart, 1987; Siegler and Robinson, 1982). In this chapter, we present a new model of early arithmetic cognition that organizes the diverse evidence on preschoolers' arithmetic abilities in terms of three fundamental components of arithmetic cognition. We argue that this model provides not only a framework for examining development within each component but also a structure for determining which processes and sequences in early arithmetic development are candidates for universals.

## A Model of Early Arithmetic Cognition

We believe that three types of knowledge underlie young children's arithmetic thinking: enumerative processes, computational procedures, and knowledge of the natural number system. Thus, each type of knowledge is represented by a component in our model of early arithmetic cognition. Together these three components constitute our most fundamental claim for universals in early arithmetic development: to the extent that arithmetic competence is present in all cultural contexts, these three components of arithmetic cognition will also be present in all cultural contexts to some degree and in some form that is consistent with their psychological definitions.

The first component, enumerative processes, entails the psychological processes children use to generate numerical representations of sets of concrete or imaginary objects. In particular, there are three enumerative processes that are present during early childhood. These include subitizing, correspondence construction, and counting. The second component, computational procedures, includes the procedures children use to perform arithmetic computations on their numerical representations of sets of objects. Our model assumes that computational procedures are specific to the enumerative process used to represent sets of objects in an arithmetic problem. Thus, each enumerative process is associated with a class of computational procedures that develop over the course of early childhood.

The third component comprises children's knowledge of the properties of the natural number system. As such, it constitutes the structural component of our model. The types of knowledge in this component include (but are not limited to) knowledge of numerical relations (for example, equivalence), knowledge of arithmetic operations (for example, addition and subtraction), and knowledge of arithmetic axioms (for example, unique sums law expressed as "equals added to equals yield equals"). This component develops over a protracted period of time as its composition changes from a presystem of arithmetic knowledge in early childhood to a system of arithmetic knowledge in later childhood and beyond. It may be noted that both the second and third components include knowledge about arithmetic transformations on sets of objects in a problem. The principal differences between them concern the nature of the numerical knowledge used in solving an arithmetic problem. The procedures comprising the second component are used to compute a numerical value (for example, a sum) for the outcome of an arithmetic transformation on a set of a specified number of objects. In contrast, the knowledge in the third component is used to reason about general relations between numbers or between arithmetic transformations in a problem.

We now present some sample protocols of children's numerical activities in order to illustrate the three components of our model. The following protocol illustrates the first component, enumerative processes. The child will use an enumerative process, counting, to form a numerical representation of a set of objects.

> J. S. (3 years, 6 months) and an interviewer are seated at a table with a puppet. The interviewer places three pennies in a single linear array in front of the puppet and asks the child how many pennies the puppet has on the table. The child points to each successive penny in the array as she counts, "one, two, three—three."

In this protocol, J. S. has used counting to form an accurate numerical representation of the set of pennies.

In the next protocol, a child uses the enumerative process of counting to solve an arithmetic problem. This protocol illustrates the second component of our model, computational procedures. The child will use her counting process in a procedure that computes the effect of an addition transformation on a set of objects.

> N. S. (5 years, 3 months) and an interviewer are seated at a table with a puppet. The interviewer places five pennies in a single linear array in front of the puppet and asks the child how many pennies the puppet has

on the table. The child points to each successive penny in the array as she counts "one, two, three, four, five—five." Then the interviewer screens the array from the child's view. Next, the interviewer says that he is going to give two more pennies to the puppet, and the child observes as the interviewer places two pennies beneath the screen. (The child does not see the outcome of this addition to the array.) The interviewer then asks the child how many pennies the puppet now has. The child holds up all five fingers on her right hand and two fingers on her left hand. She then proceeds to count onward from the last finger of her right hand and to move each successive finger as she counts it, "five, (right hand), six, seven (left hand)—seven."

Note that N. S. is using the fingers of her right hand as a symbolic vehicle to represent the five screened pennies in the initial set, and she is using two fingers of her left hand to represent the addend. She then uses an efficient procedure, called counting-on, that computes the sum without recounting the initial set.

The final protocol illustrates the third component of our model, knowledge of the natural number system. The child will use her knowledge of the inverse relation between addition and subtraction to solve an arithmetic problem.

E. H. (5 years, 10 months) and an interviewer are seated at a table. The interviewer places an unspecified number of pennies in a linear array on the table. Next, the interviewer provides the child with a container filled with pennies and asks the child to construct a second array that has the same number as the first array on the table. The child uses a one-to-one correspondence process to pair each penny from the first array with a penny from the container. The result is a second linear array (beneath the first) that is equal in number and spatial alignment to the first array. The interviewer then screens both arrays from view, removes two pennies from the container, and adds them to the first array while it is screened. The interviewer asks the child whether the arrays still have the same number, and the child answers, "No. You have more pennies in your row." The interviewer then removes the screen and asks the child to "fix the rows so that they have the same number of pennies." The child removes two pennies from the first array (although not the ones that had previously been added by the interviewer) and says, "Now the rows have the same number." The interviewer asks the child how she knows the rows have the same number, and the child answers, "At first we had the same. You put two more on yours, so I took two of yours away, and now we have the same number again."

E. H. uses her knowledge of the inverse relation between addition and subtraction to solve the problem. At no time was it necessary for her to know exactly how many pennies were in the arrays. Thus, the inverse relation applies regardless of the number of objects in the set undergoing transformation.

## Components of Early Arithmetic Cognition

*Component 1: Enumerative Processes.* The everyday world of young children presents many circumstances that call for mathematical thinking. There is numerical content in many of the books, games, and songs for young children as well as in everyday domestic activities such as the setting of places at mealtime. Furthermore, even when there is no external exigency to engage in numerical activity, young children will spontaneously enumerate a flight of stairs, objects in a counting book, or other sets of concrete objects they encounter in their environment. The first component in our model includes the psychological processes children use to form numerical representations of sets. Some of these processes can be used to enumerate not only sets of concrete objects encountered in the environment but also sets of imaginary objects, such as a set of objects that a child imagines while hearing a story or word problem. Because enumeration is important in many of the everyday affairs of societies, it is not surprising that every society has invented or adopted some conventionalized form of enumeration (Menninger [1958] 1969; Saxe and Posner, 1983; Zaslavsky, 1973). Within the first few years of life, children come to know both the universal, nonconventional aspects and the conventional aspects of enumeration. During early childhood, three enumerative processes are present: subitizing, correspondence construction, and counting. We will examine the development of each of these in turn.

*Subitizing.* There has been considerable debate about the internal nature of subitizing (Allport, 1975; Klahr, 1973; Mandler and Shebo, 1982), but there is agreement about some of its characteristics. Subitizing is thought to be a perceptual process that operates accurately and very quickly (that is, in a fraction of a second) in determining exactly how many objects are contained in a small set of objects (less than or equal to four or five). It cannot be used to enumerate large sets except when a large set has been divided into small subsets each of which is subitized and then added to a running total.

The only basic ontogenetic change in subitizing that has been documented is an extension of the range of subitizable set sizes. From infancy to age three years, infants and toddlers can only subitize sets of one to three objects. At age three, this range extends somewhat to sets of one to four (Starkey and Cooper, 1980, 1988).

Subitizing in young children is illustrated by the following study conducted by one of us and a colleague (Starkey and Cooper, 1988). In the first experimental task, we displayed one set of dots on a rear-

Table 1. Proportion of Correct Judgments in Starkey and Cooper's Subitizing Study

| Numerosity of Comparison Sets | | Age Level | | | |
|---|---|---|---|---|---|
| Standard Set | To-Be-Subitized Set | 5 years | 4 years | 3 years | 2 years |
| 1 or 2 | 1 | 1.00* | 1.00* | 1.00* | 1.00* |
| 1, 2, or 3 | 2 | 1.00* | .97* | 1.00* | .98* |
| 2, 3, or 4 | 3 | .96* | .84* | .91* | .75* |
| 3, 4, or 5 | 4 | .77* | .66* | .68* | .50 |
| 4, 5, or 6 | 5 | .54 | .57 | .58 | .50 |
| 5, 6, or 7 | 6 | .64 | .51 | .56 | - |
| 6 or 7 | 7 | .54 | .46 | .50 | - |

Note: * means $p < .05$.

projection viewing screen for 2 seconds. We then removed this set and displayed another set of dots for only 0.2 seconds, a duration whose brevity allows the use of subitizing but disallows the use of counting (Klahr and Wallace, 1976). After seeing these sets, children then told us whether they thought the sets were equal in numerosity ("the same") or unequal ("not the same"). On some trials, the sets were equal in numerosity; on the others, they differed by one dot. After completing these trials, the four- and five-year-olds participated in a second task in which we presented only a single set. Children told us how many dots they thought (or guessed) were in the set.

We found that children rarely attempted to count the sets that were displayed very briefly. In the first task, children at all levels subitized the numerically small sets and went on to correctly determine whether the sets were equal (see Table 1). Note that three-, four-, and five-year-olds were correct more often than expected by chance when one of the sets contained four or fewer dots but not when both sets contained five or more. This indicates that they could subitize sets of one to four dots but not larger sets. In the second experimental task, four- and five-year-olds correctly stated the number of dots in 90 percent of the small sets of four or fewer dots but did so on just 25 percent of the larger sets. The two-year-olds, in contrast to the older children, could subitize only sets of one to three dots. Thus, the range of subitizable sets was greater in the older children. From this study, we conclude that young children possess and spontaneously use subitizing to represent the numerosity of small sets.

Another study conducted by one of the authors (Starkey, 1987) demonstrated that young children not only can form numerical representations of sets through the use of their subitizing process, they also can retain these numerical representations in memory and can use them to reconstruct sets that have been removed from view. We discovered these competencies in young children through the use of a "searchbox" task we developed for this study. In the task, we presented children with a set of one to five identical objects (balls) and asked them first to place the set object by object into an opaque container, designated as the "searchbox." We then instructed the children to remove the entire set. The searchbox had a false floor and trap door that we could operate in such a way that only one object was actually in the main chamber of the searchbox while a child was searching inside it. The searchbox thus yielded only one object per reach into it. We recorded the number of times children reached into the searchbox to remove an object on any given trial. This indicated whether they knew how many objects should be inside.

We found that children at all age levels did know how many objects were inside if the set was small (three or fewer). Children usually were silent while performing the task. They rarely counted, nor did they make use of their fingers to stand for the screened objects. They also rarely named the objects or referred to their physical properties. These observations point to the use of numerical representations formed by subitizing rather than by one of the other enumerative processes available during early childhood. Young children use these representations to reconstruct sets they had concealed in the searchbox.

*Correspondence Construction.* Another enumerative process present during early childhood is correspondence construction. This process is used to pair each object in one set with one and only one object in another set. Correspondence construction establishes a one-to-one correspondence between objects of different sets through any of a variety of spatial relations, such as containment (in which an object of one set is placed into an object of the other set), support (in which an object of one set is placed onto an object of the other set), and adjacency (in which an object of one set is placed next to an object of the other set). This enumerative process uses one-to-one correspondence to provide information about the relative numerosity of two sets, which we can call set $A$ and set $B$. If every object in $A$ can be paired with (placed onto) one and only one object in $B$, and if every object in $B$ can be paired with one and only one object in $A$, then the sets are equal in numerosity. If every object in $A$ can be paired with one and only one object in a subset of $B$, and if every object in $B$ can not be paired with one and only one object in $A$, then the sets are unequal and set $A$ is smaller in numerosity than set $B$.

Young children who are just entering early childhood are already constructing correspondences between sets of objects in their spontaneous manipulations of objects (Langer, 1986; Sugarman, 1983). Early developments in this enumerative process are its extension from small to large sets and from two to more than two sets. Also, the types of spatial relations used in constructing correspondences increase in variety and abstraction. Two-year-olds construct correspondences only between two sets of four or fewer objects. In constructing these correspondences, they typically use either containment or support relations. Between two and three years of age, children begin to make use of a third, more abstract, spatial relation—adjacency—in which objects from one set are placed next to objects from another set without physical contact between the paired objects (Sugarman, 1983). This relation too is initially limited to children's constructions of small sets. When presented with larger sets, even four-year-olds often fail to construct a correspondence through the use of proximity.

The development of children's use of proximity to construct correspondences is illustrated in the following study by Piaget ([1941] 1952): Six bottles containing liquid and a tray holding twelve glasses are placed onto a table. The bottles are arranged such that they form a row. Piaget tells the child to look at the bottles and to imagine that they are bottles in a café. The child pretends to be a waiter and is given the task of taking glasses from the tray such that each bottle has a glass into which its contents could be poured. After the child places the chosen number of glasses in a row near the bottles, he or she is asked whether there are equal numbers of bottles and glasses. The child then watches as Piaget performs a length transformation on the row of glasses in order to determine whether the child believes that number is conserved across the transformation. This latter part of the procedure is, of course, a version of Piaget's number conservation task. It is the initial part of the procedure, however, that reveals developments in children's use of the correspondence construction process.

Piaget found that the younger children in the study, typically the four-year-olds, did not use correspondence construction to determine the number of glasses needed to construct a set that was equal in number to the set of bottles. Instead, they used figural properties such as the overall length of the rows. Therefore, they usually took an incorrect number of glasses from the tray. A child's use of figural properties is evident in the following exchange between Bon (4 years) and Experimenter (*E*) from one of Piaget's protocols:

*E:* Now put out enough glasses for the bottles, just one for each.
*(Bon then took all twelve glasses, but put them close together, so that the six bottles made a longer row.)*
*E:* Where are there more?
*Bon:* There *(the bottles).*
*E:* Well, put one glass for each bottle.
*(Bon then made the twelve glasses into a row the same length as that of the six bottles)* [Piaget, 1952, p. 43].

Older children, typically five- and six-year-olds, did use correspondence construction to determine the number of glasses needed.

Fu (5 years, 9 months) poured the liquid from six bottles into six glasses and put the glasses in front of the empty bottles [Piaget, 1952, p. 42].

It is evident from these protocols that the correspondence construction process develops over a protracted period of time. We will next examine the nature and development of the young child's counting process.

*Counting.* The third enumerative process that is present during early childhood is counting. Gelman and Gallistel (1978) describe counting as a set of principles. The central set of principles are the three how-to-count principles: (1) the one-one principle—assign one and only one distinct tag (for instance, a number name) to each object in a set as it is counted; (2) the stable order principle—the tags that are used to correspond to objects in a set must be arranged in a stable (repeatable) order; and (3) the cardinal principle—the final number name that is used in counting a set has a special significance; that is, it represents the number of objects contained in the set (for example, the cardinality of the set). An alternative characterization by Saxe (1979) emphasizes the role of operational structures in the development of counting. In Saxe's model, cognitive structural organization produces a system of coordinated operations. Specifically, the successive iteration of elements used in counting is coordinated with the progressive summation of these elements. When this coordination has been accomplished, children can utilize their society's counting system.

The counting process undergoes development throughout early childhood. Between two and three years of age, children begin to apply all three counting principles in conjunction when they count a set of objects. Two-year-olds may apply one or two principles when they attempt to count a set, but they typically do not apply all three. Second, with increasing age, young children apply the counting principles to progressively larger sets. These patterns and other aspects of early counting are illustrated in the following study.

Gelman and Gallistel (1978) presented children between two and five years of age with a standard counting task. Sets of two to nineteen objects were presented, and children were asked how many objects were in the sets. It was found that at all age levels children attempted to count at least some sets. In order to make comparisons among children's performances, the following criterion will be used: a child will be credited with a stable application of the principles if, for a given set size, the child usually (that is, on at least 60 percent of the trials) counts aloud and in conjunction with all three principles. The two-year-olds in the study did not satisfy the criterion on sets of any size. A majority of the three-year-olds met this criterion on sets containing four or fewer objects, but fewer than 30 percent did on sets containing more than five objects. Five and nine were the largest sets on which the four-year-olds and five-year-olds, respectively, satisfied the criterion. When children counted large sets incorrectly, their errors were not equally distributed across the three counting principles. The fewest errors resulted from failure to apply the stable order principle, and the most errors resulted from failure to apply the cardinal principle. One-one errors were intermediate between these two.

A developmental shift in young children's counting thus occurs between the ages of two and three years. Typically, two-year-olds do not simultaneously apply all three counting principles when they count a given set of objects, even if the set contains only a few items. Two-year-olds, as do older children, apply the stable order principle most often. The one-one principle, however, is used less often and is often violated at some point in the child's count. The cardinal principle is used least often in two-year-olds' counts and rarely accompanies the other principles.

Two-year-olds thus encounter difficulty when they attempt to coordinate different principles of counting. Gelman and Gallistel (1978) describe this deficit as failure to apply the three counting principles in conjunction. Saxe (1979) characterizes the deficit as a failure to coordinate successive iteration and progressive summation. However modeled, the basis for this deficit is not fully understood. One hypothesis is that the conceptual competence of very young children is incomplete and that cognitive structural developments result in the coordination of principles or operations of counting (Saxe, 1979). An alternative hypothesis is that the conceptual competence of very young children is complete in regard to counting but the ability to utilize this competence in some task environments is incomplete (Gelman and Meck, 1983). Thus, an integrated set of counting principles can lose its coherence in some task environments (Greeno, Riley, and Gelman, 1984). Researchers are currently attempting to determine whether and how changes in task environments influence young children's utilization of conceptual competence (Gelman and Meck, 1983; Gelman, Meck, and Merkin, 1986; Saxe, Schonfeld, and Segal [cited in Saxe, 1979]). This area of research should ultimately go a long way toward specifying the origins of the counting process and the nature of early developments in counting.

*Cross-Process Sequences.* Young children's enumerative processes form a developmental sequence. The beginnings of subitizing and correspondence construction are evident in the perceptual and action systems, respectively, of the infant. These processes can be used in some task environments from a very early point in development. Less is known about how or when the counting process originates. It is theoretically possible that counting principles are also present very early in life. Counting, however, incorporates symbols (number names or body-part symbols) into its functioning, and at the present time, there is no strong evidence that symbols are used during the first nine months or so of life. Furthermore, there are no known task environments in which children use counting principles in conjunction until age thirty to thirty-six months. Therefore, subitizing and correspondence construction appear to be used at an earlier point in development than counting.

***Component 2: Computational Procedures.*** When a set of objects is transformed by an arithmetic operation (addition), the numerosity of the set is changed. The new numerosity could be determined by reenumerating the set. For example, suppose a five-object set is transformed by the addition of two objects. The sum could be determined by counting the entire set of objects. This would be an inefficient, perhaps tedious, and certainly error-prone solution procedure, especially when large sets are involved. More efficient and accurate procedures are possible. For example, if the numerosity of a five-object set has already been determined through counting and then the set is transformed as in the example above, the sum can be determined by counting up from that cardinal value ("Five, six, seven—seven!").

After children have begun to use processes to enumerate sets of objects, they begin to use these processes to compute the effects of arithmetic transformations on sets. Young children acquire their early computational procedures outside the context of formal instruction in arithmetic problem solving. Because computational procedures develop in all children without formal instruction, we hypothesize that they are universal. Furthermore, the developmental lag between children's use of an enumerative process and their use of the associated computational procedures results from the additional and more sophisticated use of the enumerative process. We will now discuss the development of computational procedures that are associated with subitizing, correspondence construction, and counting.

*Computational Procedures Associated with Subitizing.* The earliest computational procedures that researchers have discovered are present near the beginning of early childhood. They appear to emerge in the second year of life during the transitional period between infancy and early childhood, and they are associated with subitizing. The following study by one of the authors (Starkey, 1987) illustrates the use of these early computational procedures by young children.

We used the searchbox task (described earlier) to investigate developments in young children's abilities to solve very simple addition and subtraction problems. Children between the ages of two and four years placed sets of one to five objects into the searchbox. We then either added one to four objects or subtracted one to three objects and then asked the child to remove the contents of the box. (The child did not see the set while we were transforming it, but did see how many objects were added or subtracted.)

We will first describe the findings on children's solutions to the addition problems. Because young children can subitize only small sets, we have categorized the addition problems by the numerical size of their sum. Children of all ages were correct more often than expected by chance when the sum was three or fewer but not when it was four or more. They rarely counted or named the objects they were manipulating. Subtraction problems were more difficult than addition problems: the three- and four-year-olds solved small numerosity problems that had a minuend of three or fewer (for example, 3 − 1 = __) problems, but the two-year-olds did not solve even these. Thus, addition problems were solved at an earlier age than were subtraction problems. Evidently, it is more difficult for young children to plan or execute procedures for computing answers to subtraction problems than to addition problems. Further research will be needed to specify the reasons for this.

*Computational Procedures Associated with Correspondence Construction.* In order to use the correspondence construction process to solve arithmetic problems, children must generate a procedure that manipulates correspondence relations between two sets of objects. The procedures cannot manipulate specified numerosities of the sets because the correspondence construction process only provides relational information about whether two sets are equal or unequal.

At first young children do not use correspondence construction procedures. Children younger than age five years use figural cues such as the spatial alignment of two arrays to judge whether the arrays are equal (Piaget, [1941]1952). At a later point in development, five-year-olds detect and use "gaps" in the configurations of the arrays. *Gaps* are correspondence relations between objects present in one array and objects missing in the other array. These children, however, do not use gaps in a computational procedure yet. Not until six years of age do children begin to use gaps in a correspondence construction procedure in order to solve addition and subtraction problems.

Children's use of a correspondence construction procedure is evident in a study conducted by one of the authors (Klein, 1984). Four- to six-year-old children were presented with a set of addition and subtraction problems. Each problem was presented as a pair of linear arrays of seven to ten objects (toy dinosaurs), which were placed in spatial one-to-one correspondence. Children looked at the initial pair of arrays and, without counting, judged them to be equal or judged one array to have more and then explained the basis for their judgment. Next, an addition or subtraction transformation was performed on one or both arrays, and the arrays were then screened from view. Children were asked to make a comparative numerical judgment about the screened arrays and to explain their judgment.

It was found that between five and six years of age, children began to use a correspondence construction procedure to solve the arithmetic problems. Children formed a numerical representation of the gaps in the initial pair of arrays, and after an addition or subtraction transformation was executed, they performed a numerical computation on the gaps. The following example illustrates use of this correspondence construction procedure by a six-year-old child in the study:

> The interviewer presented the child with an array of seven objects and an array of ten. The child correctly judged that the array of ten contained more than the array of seven. The interviewer then screened the arrays and added two to the smaller array. The child again correctly judged that the array of ten contained more than the other array, which contained nine (seven plus two) objects after the transformation. The child explained his judgment as follows: "Because I have three more in the beginning [referring to the gaps in the initial array of seven objects] and two left the waterhole [referring to the source set from which the two added objects were taken] to go to yours, so I have more."

Thus, six-year-olds in the study represented the initial sets by a correspondence construction process. After the addition or subtraction transformation was performed, they mentally manipulated the correspondence relations in the problem through a computational procedure.

*Computational Procedures Associated with Counting.* During early childhood, children begin to solve arithmetic problems by using computational procedures that make use of their counting process. The computational procedure used by a child on a given occasion, however, depends on the child's level of development and the task context in which the problem is presented. The importance of level of development is indicated by the developmental shift between three and four years of age in the procedures children typically use to compute the effect of an addition or subtraction transformation on a set of objects. Children who are three years of age or younger typically do not use counting procedures, whereas children who are four or older do (Siegler and Robinson, 1982; Starkey and Gelman, 1982). Three-year-olds will recount an entire set after it has been transformed if they are encouraged to count (Fuson and Hall, 1983), but in less-directed contexts, it is clear that counting is not the three-year-old's preferred manner of solution. Instead, as we saw in an earlier part of this chapter, two- and three-year-olds typically use subitizing strategies and hence correctly solve only small number problems.

Between three and four years of age, children begin to use counting procedures without being directed to count. With age, children's counting strategies become more sophisticated and efficient. For example, the counting-all strategy is replaced by the counting-on strategy ("after an addition transformation has been performed, count on from the cardinal value of the augend").

Four-year-olds use counting procedures without being directed to count. Simple reenumeration of the entire set is replaced by a counting procedure known as "counting-on." In this procedure, children solve addition problems by counting the initial set, and then after an intervening addition transformation, the child counts on from the cardinal value of the set for some number of steps equal to the addend, for example, for two steps when two objects have been added (Groen and Resnick, 1977). (A related procedure, "counting-back," which is used to solve subtraction problems, is acquired at a later age.) When sets of imaginary or screened objects are used in arithmetic problems, four- and five-year-olds still use counting procedures. In some counting procedures, fingers are held up to stand for the objects in the problem and are then counted (Siegler and Robinson, 1982). In other counting procedures, children count, perhaps from a mental image of the objects, without holding up fingers.

One of the authors and a colleague conducted a study of young children's counting procedures (Starkey and Gelman, 1982). The following examples illustrate some of the findings we have described above and demonstrate how they can be obtained: The children were between three and five years of age. We presented arithmetic problems by placing a set of pennies in one of our hands for the child to count. After a successful count, the hand was closed, screening the set from view. Next, some pennies were added to the set or subtracted from it, as in the searchbox task described earlier. Then while the transformed set remained screened from view, we asked the child how many pennies were in our hand. Three-year-olds rarely counted; they simply stated the sum, correctly or incorrectly. Four- and five-year-olds, in contrast, held up fingers to stand for the screened set of pennies and then counted their fingers, or they counted without the use of fingers or any other external props to stand for the screened set.

***Component 3: Knowledge of the Natural Number System.*** Thus far, our examination of early arithmetic cognition has revealed that young children use enumerative processes to generate numerical representations of sets of objects and that they use computational procedures to perform arithmetic computations on their numerical representations of sets. Young children's arithmetic problem solving is not limited, however, to computing specific numerical values for sets of objects or specific numerical differences between sets. In the following discussion, we argue that children also possess some knowledge of the natural number system that enables them to reason about unspecified numerical values and relations (for example, the equivalence relation between unspecified numerical values). This knowledge comprises the third component of our model of early arithmetic cognition.

What types of knowledge of the natural number system develop during early childhood? In order to answer this question, we first must define what is meant by the natural number system and the laws of such a system. The system of natural numbers is the set of positive integers from one to infinity, which corresponds to the sequence of counting tags used by children in their everyday numerical activities. An adequate characterization of the fundamental laws of a number system has long been a subject of debate among mathematicians and philosophers. Although there is currently no consensus about the laws of a formal number system, the types of knowledge included in the third component of our model are consistent with Knopp's (1952) account of arithmetic. Specifically, we propose that children's knowledge of the natural number system comprises (but is not limited to) three types: knowledge of equivalence and nonequivalence relations, knowledge of arithmetic operations, and knowledge of arithmetic axioms. We will now consider the principal developments in this component during early childhood.

One type of system knowledge that emerges early in development is knowledge of numerical relations. Children exhibit some understanding of equivalence and nonequivalence relations in particular task contexts by three (and sometimes two and a half) years of age (Gelman and Gallistel, 1978). In a series of experiments, Gelman demonstrated that preschoolers can recognize whether an equivalence or a nonequivalence relation holds between two sets of objects and, if a nonequivalence relation holds, whether these children can recognize the direction (that is, greater than or less than) of the order relation. It should be noted, however, that these experiments assessed children's knowledge of numerical relations on tasks in which the two sets being compared were small in size and were not simultaneously displayed. Thus, Piaget's ([1941] 1952) research on correspondence operations (as discussed earlier) provides an extended picture of the developments in young children's knowledge of equivalence and nonequivalence relations with respect to large sets that are simultaneously displayed in spatial relationship to each other.

Knowledge of arithmetic operations is another type of system knowledge that develops during early childhood. Recent research on children's developing concepts of addition, subtraction, division, and the inverse relation all support this conclusion. Children as young as three years of age exhibit some understanding of addition and subtraction on sets of objects whose numerical values are unspecified (Blevins-Knabe and others, 1987; Brush, 1978; Cooper and others, 1978). Their understanding of addition and subtraction, however, is limited to directional reasoning about these operations: addition to a set yields more, and subtraction from a set yields less (Klein, 1984). Children's understanding of division also develops during the toddler and preschool years. Studies have revealed that by age three years, toddlers are able to divide small sets of objects into two equal sets, even without explicit directions to do so (Klein and Langer, 1987). Further developments in children's understanding of division include preschoolers' ability to share a large set of objects equally among more than two recipients (Frydman and Bryant, in press). Finally, there is evidence that young children possess some understanding of the inverse relation between addition and subtraction, but their understanding is neither precise nor exclusively based on unspecified numerical values (Gelman and Gallistel, 1978; Klein, 1984).

The preceding evidence on young children's knowledge of numerical relations and arithmetic operations constitutes an impressive repertoire of early arithmetic abilities. Nonetheless, there are some important gaps in their knowledge of the natural number system. Most notably, research has found that the following arithmetic abilities emerge later in development, after six or seven years of age: knowledge of infinity (Gelman, 1980), knowledge of commutativity (Gréco, 1962), and knowledge of arithmetic axioms such as the unique sums law (Inhelder and Piaget, 1963). We characterize young children's arithmetic knowledge as a "presystem" because it is incomplete with respect to several fundamental properties. Nevertheless, we believe that it is a necessary precursor to the development of a more complete system of arithmetic knowledge.

**Cultural Variations and Cultural Universals**

We now will consider findings from other sociocultural contexts as they bear on the generality of the processes and developmental sequences of arithmetic cognition. Many of our remarks are speculative in nature, because relatively little cross-cultural research has been conducted on this important topic. We also will use theoretical criteria in distinguishing universal processes and developments from cultural variations in processes and developments. We will hypothesize that some underlying forms and developmental sequences are invariant and hence universal and that some surface forms and developmental rates are variable across sociocultural setting. We also propose that to the extent that arithmetic competence is present in all cultural contexts, the three general types of knowledge in our model—enumerative processes, computational procedures, and knowledge of the natural number system—will be present to some degree and in some form.

*Knowledge of the Natural Number System.* Only a brief examination of the natural number system is warranted, given the sparseness of the developmental cross-cultural data on this important topic. We believe that the presystem form of this knowledge is universal.

Two studies bear on this issue. Pettito and Ginsburg (1982) found that unschooled Dioula (Ivory Coast) adults use some arithmetic axioms, but perhaps not others, in solving arithmetic problems. Ginsburg and Russell (1981) observed that knowledge of the inverse develops more slowly in lower-class children than in middle-class children. We know of no other study that has investigated knowledge of the natural number system in young children across sociocultural contexts.

***Enumerative Processes and Computational Procedures.*** There is considerable evidence that children from a number of sociocultural contexts enumerate sets of objects and use computational procedures to determine the effects of arithmetic transformations on these sets. The use of enumerative processes and computational procedures by poor and by working-class children (Ginsburg and Russell, 1981; Saxe, Guberman, and Gearhart, 1987) and by children from a variety of Third World settings (Posner, 1982; Saxe, 1981a) have been documented. Subitizing, correspondence construction and counting have been observed across sociocultural contexts. However, sociocultural variables can influence the surface forms of some of these processes.

*Subitizing.* The evidence indicates that the genesis and development of subitizing occur naturally, without culturally specific supports, in all constitutionally normal children. Subitizing has been found in children from non-Western societies (Posner, 1982). It is present in middle-class, Western infants (Antell and Keating, 1983; Starkey and Cooper, 1980; Strauss and Curtis, 1984), and a form of it has been observed in non-human primates (Klein and Starkey, 1987). The form of subitizing in children is probably invariant across sociocultural contexts, because it is a perceptual process that requires no special cultural supports. Small sets are omnipresent in the environment of every child and thus are readily available to the process. After subitizing has been used to detect the numerosity of a set, the perceiver may then use a symbol such as a general purpose number name (two, *dos*), a special purpose number name (quartet, yoke), or a manual gesture (as in American sign language) to refer to the numerosity. The symbols that are used to refer to subitized numerosities vary with sociocultural setting (Wertheimer, 1938). We know of no cross-cultural findings on the development of subitizing or on the use of this process in arithmetic problem solving, but for many of the reasons that we believe subitizing to be invariant in form, we also hypothesize that it is used by all children in similar ways to solve arithmetic problems.

*Correspondence Construction.* Correspondence construction, like subitizing, is a universal enumerative process. Correspondence construction has been observed in many cross-cultural studies of number conservation (Ashton, 1975; Dasen, 1977). Its genesis occurs early in development: it has been traced back to the sensorimotor activity of infants reared in middle-class, Western settings (Langer, 1980; Sinclair and others, 1982). A form of correspondence construction has been observed in nonhuman primates (Klein and Starkey, 1987). The surface form of correspondence construction varies across sociocultural contexts. A variety of tally sticks and other devices that are used to establish numerical correspondences are present in many cultures (Menninger, [1958] 1969).

We are aware of only one developmental study that has to any extent examined the use of correspondence construction to solve arithmetic problems in other sociocultural contexts (Ginsburg and Russell, 1981). This study found that lower-class Western children could solve some problems. We cannot generalize from a single study; however, there is further reason to believe that computational procedures will develop in children of other cultures. Middle-class, Western children begin using correspondence construction computationally without any formal schooling. Also, children in other sociocultural contexts possess a correspondence construction process, and they come to conserve numbers (Ashton, 1975; Dasen, 1977). The latter finding is pertinent, because some of the knowledge that is required to solve Piaget's standard number conservation problem is also required in the use of correspondence construction to solve arithmetic problems.

We expect differences in the rate of development of computational procedures that employ correspondence construction due to environmental variables, such as a curriculum or trade in which such knowledge is helpful. Ginsburg and Russell (1981) found that the rates of development of arithmetic problem solving and number conservation from preschool to kindergarten age were slower in lower-class than in middle-class children. In addition, cross-cultural research has revealed differences in the rate of development of enumeration by correspondence construction and of number conservation (Posner and Baroody, 1979).

*Counting.* Counting is also a universal enumerative process. Some form of counting has been discovered in virtually every culture (Saxe and Posner, 1983; Zaslavsky, 1973). The use of computational procedures to solve arithmetic problems has also been discovered in different sociocultural settings (Ginsburg and Russell, 1981; Saxe, 1981b). Counting systems differ in the type of symbol they employ and in the base structure they code in the symbol. Middle-class Western children employ number names (one, two, twenty-two) as symbols that code a base ten structure. In contrast, Oksapmin children of Papua New Guinea employ body parts (the right thumb, right index finger, left wrist) as symbols that code no base structure (Lancy, 1983; Saxe and Posner, 1983). These are only superficial differences between the two counting systems. An underlying similarity is that both honor the set of counting principles.

Superficially different counting systems pose special problems to young children who are acquiring them. For example, Oksapmin children sometimes confuse physically similar body parts (left elbow and right elbow), which can be problematic because these body parts stand for different numerical magnitudes (Saxe, 1981a). Sociocultural differences in rate of development of counting and of counting procedures used to solve arithmetic problems have been documented (Ginsburg and Russell, 1981; Saxe, 1981b; Song and Ginsburg, 1987).

## Conclusion

Our central concern in this chapter has been to specify those aspects of early arithmetic development that are universal across sociocultural contexts. The most fundamental claim we make in this regard is that the three components of our model are universally present to some extent and in some form. In addition to this, we argue that universals are present within each component. Within the first component, the underlying forms of subitizing, correspondence construction, and counting are universal enumerative processes, and the cross-process sequence (for example, the use of subitizing and correspondence construction prior to the use of counting) comprises a universal developmental sequence. Within the second component, the use of subitizing, correspondence construction, and counting procedures in arithmetic problem solving is universal, and the emergence of an enumerative process prior to the emergence of associated computational procedures comprises a type of developmental sequence that is universal. Finally, within the third component, the presystem form of knowledge of the natural number system is universal across sociocultural context.

Our examination of research findings on early arithmetic cognition in various sociocultural settings provides varying amounts of support for the universals we have hypothesized. There is a clear need for further research that is systematic and comprehensive in regard to the components we have outlined here.

## References

Allport, D. A. "The State of Cognitive Psychology." *Quarterly Journal of Experimental Psychology*, 1975, *27*, 141-152.

Antell, S. R., and Keating, D. "Perception of Numerical Invariance by Neonates." *Child Development*, 1983, *54*, 695-701.

Ashton, P. "Cross-Cultural Piagetian Research: An Experimental Perspective." *Harvard Educational Review*, 1975, *45*, 475-506.

Blevins-Knabe, B., Cooper, R. G., Mace, P. G., Starkey, P., and Leitner, E. "Preschoolers Sometimes Know Less Than We Think: The Use of Quantifiers to Solve Addition and Subtraction Tasks." *Bulletin of the Psychonomic Society*, 1987, *25*, 31-34.

Brush, L. R. "Preschool Children's Knowledge of Addition and Subtraction." *Journal for Research in Mathematics Education*, 1978, *9*, 44-54.

Cooper, R. G., Starkey, P., Blevins, B., Goth, P., and Leitner, E. "Number Development: Addition and Subtraction." Paper presented at the meeting of the Jean Piaget Society, Philadelphia, 1978.

Dasen, P. R. *Piagetian Psychology: Cross-Cultural Contributions*. New York: Gardner, 1977.

Frydman, O., and Bryant, P. "Sharing and the Understanding of Number Equivalence by Young Children." *Cognitive Development*, in press.

Fuson, K. C., and Hall, J. W. "The Acquisition of Early Number Word Meanings:

A Conceptual Analysis and Review." In H. P. Ginsburg (ed.), *The Development of Mathematical Thinking.* Orlando, Fla.: Academic Press, 1983.

Gelman, R. "What Young Children Know About Numbers." *Educational Psychologist,* 1980, *15,* 54-68.

Gelman, R., and Gallistel, C. R. *The Child's Understanding of Number.* Cambridge, Mass.: Harvard University Press, 1978.

Gelman, R., and Meck, E. "Preschoolers' Counting: Principles Before Skill." *Cognition,* 1983, *13,* 343-359.

Gelman, R., Meck, E., and Merkin, S. "Young Children's Numerical Competence." *Cognitive Development,* 1986, *1,* 1-29.

Ginsburg, H. P., and Russell, R. L. "Social Class and Racial Influences on Early Mathematical Thinking." *Monographs of the Society for Research in Child Development,* 1981, *46* (6), serial no. 193.

Gréco, P. "Une recherche sur la commutativité de l'addition" [An investigation into the commutativity of addition]. In P. Gréco and A. Morf (eds.), *Etudes d'épistémologie génétique.* Vol. 13: *Structures numériques élémentaires* [Studies of genetic epistemology. Vol. 13: Elementary numerical structures]. Paris: Presses Universitaires de France, 1962.

Greeno, J. G., Riley, M. S., and Gelman, R. "Conceptual Competence and Children's Counting." *Cognitive Psychology,* 1984, *16,* 94-143.

Groen, G. J., and Resnick, L. B. "Can Preschool Children Invent Addition Algorithms?" *Journal of Educational Psychology,* 1977, *69,* 645-652.

Inhelder, B., and Piaget, J. "De l'itération des actions à la récurrence élémentaire" [From the iteraction of actions to elementary recurrence]. In P. Gréco, B. Inhelder, B. Matalon, and J. Piaget (eds.), *Etudes d'épistémologie génétique.* Vol. 17: *La formation des raisonnements récurrentiels* [Studies of genetic epistemology. Vol. 17: The formation of recurrental reasonings]. Paris: Presses Universitaires de France, 1963.

Klahr, D. "A Production System for Counting, Subitizing, and Adding." In W. G. Chase (ed.), *Visual Information Processing.* Orlando, Fla.: Academic Press, 1973.

Klahr, D., and Wallace, J. G. *Cognitive Development, an Information Processing View.* Hillsdale, N.J.: Erlbaum, 1976.

Klein, A. "The Early Development of Arithmetic Reasoning: Numerative Activities and Logical Operations." *Dissertation Abstracts International,* 1984, *45,* 375B-376B.

Klein, A., and Langer, J. "Elementary Numerical Constructions by Toddlers." Paper presented at the meeting of the Society for Research in Child Development, Baltimore, Md., 1987.

Klein, A., and Starkey, P. "The Origins and Development of Numerical Cognition: A Comparative Analysis." In J. Sloboda and D. Rogers (eds.), *Cognitive Processes in Mathematics.* Oxford, England: Oxford University Press, 1987.

Knopp, K. *Elements of the Theory of Functions.* New York: Dover, 1952.

Lancy, D. F. *Cross-Cultural Studies in Cognition and Mathematics.* Orlando, Fla.: Academic Press, 1983.

Langer, J. *The Origins of Logic: Six to Twelve Months.* Orlando, Fla.: Academic Press, 1980.

Langer, J. *The Origins of Logic: One to Two Years.* Orlando, Fla.: Academic Press, 1986.

Mandler, G., and Shebo, B. J. "Subitizing: An Analysis of Its Component Processes." *Journal of Experimental Psychology: General,* 1982, *111,* 1-22.

Menninger, K. *Number Words and Number Symbols: A Cultural History of Number.* Cambridge, Mass.: MIT Press, 1969. (Originally published 1958.)

Pettito, A. L., and Ginsburg, H. P. "Mental Arithmetic in Africa and America: Strategies, Principles, and Explanations." *International Journal of Psychology*, 1982, *17*, 81-102.

Piaget, J. *The Child's Conception of Number*. New York: Norton, 1952. (Originally published 1941.)

Posner, J. "The Development of Mathematical Knowledge in Two West African Societies." *Child Development*, 1982, *53*, 200-208.

Posner, J., and Baroody, A. "Number Conservation in Two West African Societies." *Journal of Cross-Cultural Psychology*, 1979, *10*, 479-496.

Saxe, G. B. "Developmental Relations Between Notational Counting and Number Conservation." *Child Development*, 1979, *50*, 180-187.

Saxe, G. B. "Body Parts as Numerals: A Developmental Analysis of Numeration Among the Oksapmin in Papua New Guinea." *Child Development*, 1981a, *52*, 306-316.

Saxe, G. B. "Social Change and Cognitive Growth: The Invention of Body Part Algorithms Among Oksapmin Children in Papua New Guinea." Paper presented at the 1981 biennial meeting of the Society for Research in Child Development, Boston, Mass., 1981b.

Saxe, G. B., Guberman, S. R., and Gearhart, M. "Social Processes in Early Number Development." *Monographs of the Society for Research in Child Development*, 1987, *52* (2), serial no. 216.

Saxe, G. B., and Posner, J. "The Development of Numerical Cognition: Cross-Cultural Perspectives." In H. P. Ginsburg (ed.), *The Development of Mathematical Thinking*. Orlando, Fla.: Academic Press, 1983.

Siegler, R. S., and Robinson, M. "The Development of Numerical Understandings." In H. W. Reese and L. P. Lipsitt (eds.), *Advances in Child Development and Behavior*. Vol. 16. Orlando, Fla.: Academic Press, 1982.

Sinclair, H., Stambak, M., Lézine, I., Rayna, S., and Verba, M. *Les bébés et les choses* [Babies and things]. Paris: Presses Universitaires de France, 1982.

Song, M., and Ginsburg, H. P. "The Development of Informal and Formal Mathematical Thinking in Korean and U.S. Children." *Child Development*, 1987, *59*, 1286-1296.

Starkey, P. "Early Arithmetic Competencies." Paper presented at the meeting of the Society for Research in Child Development, Baltimore, Md., 1987.

Starkey, P., and Cooper, R. G. "Perception of Numbers by Human Infants." *Science*, 1980, *210*, 1033-1035.

Starkey, P., and Cooper, R. G. "Number Perception in Preschool Children: The Development of Subitizing." Unpublished manuscript, University of California, Berkeley, 1988.

Starkey, P., and Gelman, R. "The Development of Addition and Subtraction Abilities Prior to Formal Schooling in Arithmetic." In T. P. Carpenter, J. M. Moser, and T. A. Romberg (eds.), *Addition and Subtraction: A Cognitive Perspective*. Hillsdale, N.J.: Erlbaum, 1982.

Strauss, M. S., and Curtis, L. E. "Development of Numerical Concepts in Infancy." In C. Sophian (ed.), *The Origins of Cognitive Skills*. Hillsdale, N.J.: Erlbaum, 1984.

Sugarman, S. *Children's Early Thought: Developments in Classification*. New York: Cambridge University Press, 1983.

Vygotsky, L. S. "Mind in Society: The Development of Higher Psychological Processes." In M. Cole, V. John-Steiner, S. Scribner, and E. Souberman (eds., trans.), *Mind in Society: The Development of Higher Psychological Processes*. Cambridge, Mass.: Harvard University Press, 1978.

Wertheimer, M. "Numbers and Numerical Concepts in Primitive Peoples." In W. D. Ellis (ed.), *A Source Book of Gestalt Psychology*. Boston: Routledge & Kegan Paul, 1938.

Zaslavsky, C. *Africa Counts: Number and Pattern in African Culture*. Westport, Conn.: Lawrence Hill, 1973.

*Alice Klein is research associate at the Institute of Human Development at the University of California, Berkeley. Her interests include early cognitive and perceptual development.*

*Prentice Starkey is assistant professor of education at the University of California, Berkeley. His interests include early cognitive development and its relation to education.*

*Differences across cultures in classroom instruction may contribute to superior performance by Asian children on mathematics achievement tests.*

# Mathematics Learning in Japanese, Chinese, and American Classrooms

*James W. Stigler, Michelle Perry*

It might at first glance seem misguided to study cultural differences in learning by focusing on schools. Indeed, the surface features of school mathematics are more similar than different when compared across cultures, and even classrooms in different cultures appear to resemble one another in many respects. Yet schooling is a cultural institution, and more detailed analysis reveals the subtle and pervasive effects of culture as it impinges on children's learning of school mathematics—in the

---

This paper was written while the first author was supported by a Spencer Fellowship from the National Academy of Education, and the second author by funds from the Benton Center for Curriculum and Instruction, University of Chicago. Research reported here was conducted in collaboration with Harold Stevenson, Center for Human Growth and Development, University of Michigan, and with numerous other colleagues: Shin-ying Lee, University of Michigan; Chen-chin Hsu, National Taiwan University Medical College; Lian-wen Mao, Taipei Bureau of Education, Taiwan; and Seiro Kitamura, S. Kimura, and T. Kato, Tohoku Fukushi College, Sendai, Japan. The first University of Michigan study was supported by NIMH grants MH 33259 and MH 30567, and the second by National Science Foundation grant BNS8409372. Address correspondence to: Jim Stigler, Department of Behavioral Sciences, University of Chicago, 5730 S. Woodlawn Avenue, Chicago, Illinois 60637.

curriculum, in the organization and functioning of the classroom, and in the beliefs and attitudes about learning mathematics that prevail among parents and teachers. In this chapter, we will present some of what we have learned about the classrooms in which children learn mathematics in Japan, Taiwan, and the United States.

The decision to compare mathematics learning in Asian and American classrooms is, of course, not arbitrary. We have known for some time now that American secondary school students compare poorly on tests of mathematics achievement with students from many other countries, but especially with students from Japan (Husen, 1967; McKnight and others, 1987; Travers and others, 1985). More recently, Asian-American differences in achievement have been found to exist as early as kindergarten and to be dramatic by the time children reach fifth grade. Stevenson, Lee, and Stigler (1986), for example studied children from representative samples of fifth-grade classrooms in Sendai, Japan; Taipei, Taiwan; and Minneapolis, U.S.A. On a test of mathematics achievement, the highest-scoring American classroom did not perform as well as the lowest-scoring Japanese classroom, and outperformed only one of the twenty classrooms in Taipei. Explaining differences as dramatic as these presents a challenge to researchers and also to educators who must grapple with the problem of declining mathematical competence in American society.

Where should we look for explanations? The fundamental problem we encounter is that almost every dimension on which we could compare Asian countries with the United States proves to differentiate these societies. Given this enormous confounding of factors, it is almost impossible to tell which are causally related to differences in learning and which are only related by chance. Aside from this limitation, however, there is a great deal to learn by understanding the way cultural and educational resources are marshalled to produce the outstanding achievement—at least in the domain of mathematics—produced by Asian societies. In this chapter we focus on classrooms, because classrooms are where most people learn most of what they ever know about mathematics.

Just sitting in a Japanese mathematics lesson can provide us with important insights, not only about the way mathematics is taught in Japan but also about the way mathematics is taught in the United States. We can illustrate this point with an anecdote. Several years ago we visited a mathematics class in a Japanese elementary school where the lesson was on drawing cubes in three-dimensional perspective. The class was typical by Japanese standards: thirty to forty students at their desks arranged in rows, facing the teacher who was standing at the front of the room. Each student was working in his or her notebook, but there also was a great deal of discussion from desk to desk, and the noise level was rather high. The discussions were not inappropriate, however; rather, they were directed almost completely to the mathematical topic at hand.

Against this background, one child was having trouble. His cube looked crooked, no matter how carefully he tried to copy the lines from the teacher's example. And so the teacher asked this child to go to the blackboard and draw his cube. Standing there, in front of the class, he labored to draw a cube correctly while the rest of the students in the class continued working at their desks. After working for five or ten minutes, he asked the teacher to look at his product. The teacher turned to the class and asked, "Is this correct?" The child's classmates shook their heads and said, "No, not really." After some open discussion of where the problem might lie, the child was told to continue working at the blackboard and try again. This scene continued for the duration of the forty-minute class. As the lesson progressed, the group of American observers began to feel more and more uncomfortable and anxious on behalf of the child at the board. We thought that any minute he might burst into tears, and we wondered what he must be feeling. Yet he did not cry and, in fact, did not seem at all disturbed by his plight. At the end of the class he finally drew a passable cube, in response to which the class applauded.

As we later came to learn, scenes like this are not unusual in Japanese classrooms, and later we will show how this one fits into the broader context of mathematics learning in Japan. For now, we want to focus on the effect the experience had on us, because it exemplifies one of the greatest benefits of cross-cultural research for the study of educational processes. When educational researchers look only at classrooms in their own culture, they become accustomed to many of the most predominant characteristics of those classrooms and thus fail to note the significance of those characteristics. American teachers generally do not call children to the board to display their errors, because they fear the possible damage it might do the child's self-esteem. Yet nothing drives us to question this aspect of American teaching more than to be confronted with it in a scenario like the one we have described. The anthropologist Melford Spiro (in press) has described the aim of anthropology as to make the strange familiar and the familiar strange. Nothing could better describe the aim of our research. We hope that our comparisons of Asian and American mathematics education will lead us to question practices that we take for granted and understand practices that we at first find strange.

The information about Japanese, Chinese, and American classrooms we present below comes from two large cross-cultural studies based at the University of Michigan that have investigated academic achievement and its correlates in Japan, Taiwan, and the United States. Data for the two studies were collected in 1979–80 and in 1985–86, and data from the second study are still in the process of being analyzed. Although both of these studies included testing of children and interviewing of parents as part of their designs, we will focus in this chapter on classroom observations. The methods used for observing classrooms differed substantially across the two studies. Yet taken together, they provide us with an integrated view of how mathematics classrooms differ across these three cultures.

**Differences in Mathematical Knowledge**

A criticism often voiced in response to our first study was that our test measured mostly computational skills and did not measure abilities that American educators consider to be more important, such as creative problem-solving skills. In our second study we took heed of such criticism by designing tests to sample as wide a variety of mathematical skills and knowledge as possible, thus broadening our understanding of what specific knowledge differences underlie Asian superiority in mathematics achievement. In addition to group tests of computational skills and, for fifth-grade students, basic knowledge of geometry, we constructed ten more tests of mathematics-related knowledge that were administered in two separate individual testing sessions. All of the tests were especially constructed for this study and were judged culturally unbiased by a team of researchers representing each of the cultures being studied. The tests included novel word problems, conceptual knowledge, operations, graphing, estimation, measurement, visualization, mental image transformation, mental calculation, and memory for numbers. A total of 5,524 children across a total of 160 first- and fifth-grade classrooms in the three locations were tested.

Are differences in performance restricted to computational skills, or do Asian students also do better than their American counterparts on tests of other mathematics-related skills? Although we are just beginning our analyses of the test data, the answer is clear: Japanese students, in both first and fifth grades, outscore American students on almost every test we constructed. The pattern of results from Taiwan resembled those from Japan for fifth-graders but were more mixed for first-graders. Let us briefly examine some of these results.

In Figure 1 we present box plots (Tukey, 1977) showing the distribution of school means for five representative tests from the battery. These plots are useful because they indicate both median performance (denoted by the center line) and variability across schools in each of the three locations at both grade levels. The five tests presented in Figure 1 cover a broad range of topics: (1) a test of computational skill; (2) a test of word-problem solving, including both standard and nonstandard types of problems; (3) an intensive interview designed to tap children's conceptual knowledge of mathematics across a wide variety of domains, including place value, equations, and fractions; (4) a test of estimation skills; and (5) a test requiring students to mentally fold an irregularly shaped piece of paper in accordance with verbal instructions.

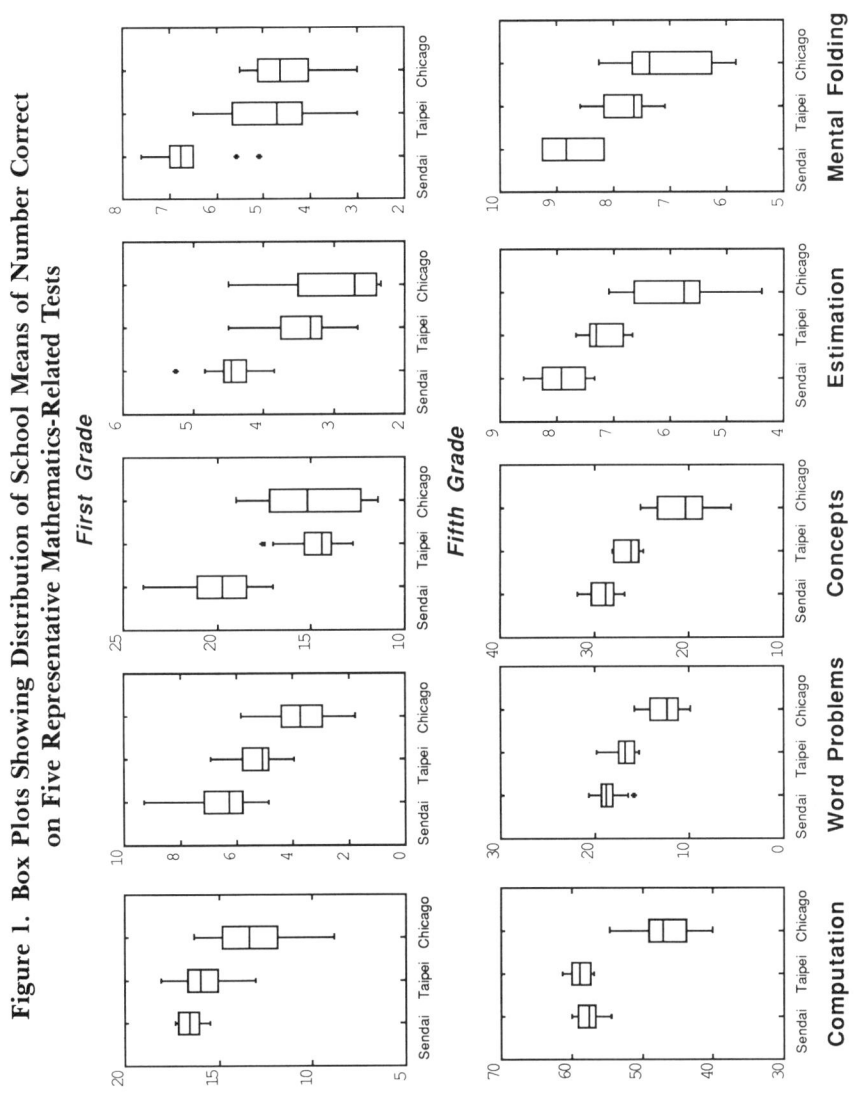

Figure 1. Box Plots Showing Distribution of School Means of Number Correct on Five Representative Mathematics-Related Tests

At the left-hand side of Figure 1 are the results of the test of computational skills. These results replicate those found in our earlier study (Stigler, Lee, Lucker, and Stevenson, 1982), even though the American children were sampled from Chicago instead of Minneapolis. At first grade, the Japanese and Chinese schools both score higher and are less variable than are the American schools, and this pattern is even more pronounced in the fifth grade. Moving to the right, we see a similar pattern for performance on the test of word problems. It is important to note that by the time students reach the fifth grade, there is almost no overlap in the distributions of Asian and American students.

The next three tests presented in Figure 1—conceptual knowledge, estimation, and mental folding—differ from the first two in that they are made up of questions not typically encountered as part of the mathematics curricula in any of the three locations. Interestingly, they also show a different pattern of results than we saw in the tests of computation and word problems. In first grade, students in Sendai are scoring far higher than are students in either Taipei or Chicago, who are performing approximately equally well. By the time they reach fifth grade, however, the students from Taiwan have passed their American counterparts and are approaching the level of performance attained by the Japanese.

In summary, the Asian advantage in mathematics, at least at the elementary school level, is not restricted to narrow domains of computation but rather pervades all aspects of mathematical reasoning. These findings should provide ample motivation for examining cultural differences in the way mathematics is learned in Japanese, Chinese, and American classrooms.

## Methods for Classroom Observations

*First Study.* The first study was conducted with a sample of first- and fifth-grade elementary school students and teachers in Sendai, Japan; Taipei, Taiwan; and the Minneapolis metropolitan area. In each city, ten representative schools were selected, and within each school two first- and two fifth-grade classrooms participated, yielding a total of 120 classrooms across the three cities. Each classroom was visited forty times over a two- to four-week period. The visits were scheduled to yield a stratified random sample of time across the school day and school week, thus making it possible to estimate the amount or percentage of time that was devoted to various activities. (A full description of the method can be found in Stigler, Lee, and Stevenson, 1987.)

Each visit lasted about an hour and included time for separate observations of teachers and of individual students. We used a time-sampling procedure to observe the target—either teacher or child—for ten seconds, and then to spend the next ten seconds coding the presence or absence of a checklist of categories. This procedure was repeated according to a predefined sequence that counterbalanced order of observation across the teacher and the twelve randomly chosen target students in each class. Across the two- to four-week observation period, each of the twelve children in each classroom was observed for about thirty-three minutes (not including coding time), and each teacher was observed for about 120 minutes.

The student coding system included thirty categories, although coding was eased somewhat by the fact that many of the categories were mutually exclusive. Various aspects of the classroom were coded from the target child's point of view, including the following: whether the class engaged in academic activities or in transition between activities, what subject matter was being taught, how the classroom was organized and who the leader was of the child's activity, and what kinds of on- and off-task behaviors the child was engaged in.

The teacher coding system contained nineteen categories. These categories described who the teacher was working with, what kinds of teaching behaviors the teacher was engaged in, and what kinds of feedback the teacher was offering to the students. Specific categories from the student and teacher coding schemes will be introduced as the results are presented.

*Second Study.* The second study was again conducted in Sendai, Japan, and Taipei, Taiwan. In the United States, however, we decided to move our study to the Chicago metropolitan area, which is far more diverse in population than Minneapolis and thus more representative of mainstream America. In each of the two Asian cities, ten schools were selected to participate in the study. In the Chicago area, twenty schools were chosen to represent the urban and suburban areas that make up Cook County. Twenty rather than ten schools were chosen, because Cook County is more diverse than either of the Asian cities. Within our Chicago sample, we included public and private schools; upper, middle, and lower socioeconomic status neighborhoods; predominantly black, white, Hispanic, and mixed ethnic schools; and urban and suburban environments. As in the first study, two first-grade and two fifth-grade classrooms from each school were selected to participate in the study, yielding a total sample of 160 classrooms in the three locations.

Observations for the second study differed in two important ways from observations conducted in the first study. First, only mathematics classes were observed. Second, detailed narrative descriptions of each class were recorded, yielding a far richer source of information than we had available from the first study.

Each of the 160 classrooms in the mathematics study was visited four separate times over a one- to two-week period, yielding a total of 640 observations across the three locations. Observers, who were local residents of each city, arrived just before teachers began the daily mathematics lesson and observed until the mathematics class was over.

The observers were instructed to write down as much as they could about what was transpiring during the class. Their goal was to record the ongoing flow of behaviors and to include descriptions of all supporting materials (for example, what was written on the blackboard, how many children were working on which problem, and so on). The observers also noted, with marks in the margin, when each minute of time had elapsed. These minute markers were included so that we would be able to estimate the duration of various activities.

The observations produced 640 different narrative descriptions of mathematics classes, in three different languages. Not all observations were of equal quality: the observations varied in both detail and consistency. How were we to code and summarize the data into a form that would be useful in characterizing cross-cultural differences in mathematics teaching?

We first convened a group of bi- and tri-lingual coders to read all of the observations and to summarize their contents in English. In addition, a subset of the observations was translated verbatim into English. From these, we developed a feel for the range of situations we would have to code and some intuitions about cross-cultural differences. We then constructed a coding system that contained some predefined categories but that also included procedures that would preserve detail.

Each observation was divided into segments as the basic unit of analysis. A segment was defined as changing if there was a change in either topic, materials, or activity. Topics were globally defined, including categories such as telling time, measurement, or addition facts. Materials included such items as textbooks, worksheets, the blackboard, or flashcards. Activities, again, were rather molar: examples included seatwork, students solving problems on the blackboard, or teachers giving explanations. The categories were not intended as the full description of the class but rather as a way of organizing the information into a more useful format. As it turned out, there were not large cross-cultural differences in either the average number of segments that comprised a lesson (five to six segments in first grade, six to eight in fifth grade), or the average duration of each segment (seven to eight minutes in first grade, five to six in fifth grade).

In addition, an English language summary was constructed of each segment that would recapitulate in some detail what was going on during the segment. The summaries were standardized somewhat by the use of keywords that would alert us to the presence or absence of certain categories in the classroom. For example, whenever a student was observed asking a question of the teacher, the summary would include the standard keyword "S-to-T," which would facilitate a computer search for all such situations. Our goal was to make the summaries as consistent as possible in style and language.

**Time, Organization, and Disorganization: Findings from the Objective Coding**

The results of the first observational study served mainly to differentiate classrooms in the United States, on one hand, from classrooms in Japan and Taiwan, on the other. Very few differences emerged between Chinese and Japanese classrooms. In some respects, one only has to visit one Chinese or Japanese classroom to see vast differences between Asian and American elementary school classrooms. Class size is a major difference: while the classrooms in our Minneapolis sample average twenty-two students in the first grade and twenty-four students in the fifth grade, the classrooms in Taipei average forty-five and forty-eight students at the two grade levels, and those in Sendai, thirty-nine at both grade levels. Most Asian classrooms are arranged with desks in rows facing the teacher, while American classrooms often have desks arranged in groups.

The two dimensions on which the Asian observations differed most from the American ones were time spent in the teaching and learning of mathematics and the level of organization in the classroom.

*Time.* Children in Japan and Taiwan spend significantly more time in school than do American children, and this ultimately translates into significantly more time learning mathematics. School is in session 240 days per year in both Japan and Taiwan, compared to only 180 days per year in the United States. Although first-graders in all three cities that we studied spent about thirty hours per week in school, fifth-graders in Sendai spent thirty-seven hours a week in school, those in Taipei, forty-four hours, and those in Minneapolis still only thirty hours.

During academic classes, Chinese and Japanese children at both grade levels spent a much higher percentage of their time engaged in academic activities than did American children. In first grade, American, Chinese, and Japanese children spent 69.8 percent, 85.1 percent, and 79.2 percent of the time, respectively, engaged in academic activities. At the fifth grade the corresponding percentages were 64.5 percent, 91.5 percent, and 87.4 percent. Furthermore, although the percentage increased between first and fifth grade for the Asian children, the percentage actually declined slightly across grade levels for the American children.

The majority of class time in all three cultures was devoted to either reading/language arts or mathematics, and although the total percentage of time devoted to either one of these subject matters was similar across the three cultures, the way time was apportioned between the two varied significantly by culture. American teachers at both grade levels devoted more time to reading/language arts and less time to mathematics than

Table 1. Number of Hours Each Week Spent
in Language Arts and Mathematics

|  | U.S.A. | Country Taiwan | Japan |
|---|---|---|---|
| First Grade |  |  |  |
| Language arts | 10.6 | 10.5 | 8.8 |
| Mathematics | 2.9 | 3.9 | 6.0 |
| Fifth Grade |  |  |  |
| Language arts | 8.2 | 11.2 | 7.8 |
| Mathematics | 3.4 | 11.4 | 7.6 |

did Chinese and Japanese teachers. By the fifth grade, both Chinese and Japanese teachers spent approximately equal time teaching mathematics and reading. American teachers, by contrast, spent almost three times as much time on reading as they did on mathematics.

Calculations based on the hours per week spent in school, the percentage of time spent in academic activities, and the percentage of time those academic activities were mathematics versus reading/language arts allow us to estimate the number of hours each week children in the three cultures spend working on the different subject matters. The results of these calculations are presented in Table 1. The cross-cultural differences in the number of hours devoted to mathematics instruction are large, sufficiently large, in fact, that they could go a long way toward explaining the cross-cultural differences in mathematics achievement.

*Organization.* The second dimension that differentiated American mathematics classrooms from those in Japan and Taiwan was the way in which the classrooms were organized. Classrooms in Japan and Taiwan were centrally organized, with most activity under the direct control and supervision of the teacher, while classrooms in the United States were more decentralized in their structure and functioning. Correlated with this difference in type of organization was a difference in the amount of disorderly, off-task behavior present in the classrooms, such that the American classrooms, where there was less direct control by the teacher, also evidenced more off-task behavior.

These differences in type of classroom organization were indexed by several categories in our observational coding scheme. The upper panel of Figure 2 shows the level of organization of the classroom as coded in the observations of children. Japanese and Chinese students spent the vast majority of their time working, watching, and listening together as a class and were rarely divided into smaller groups. American children, by contrast, spent the majority of their time working on their own and a smaller amount of time working in activities as a member of the whole

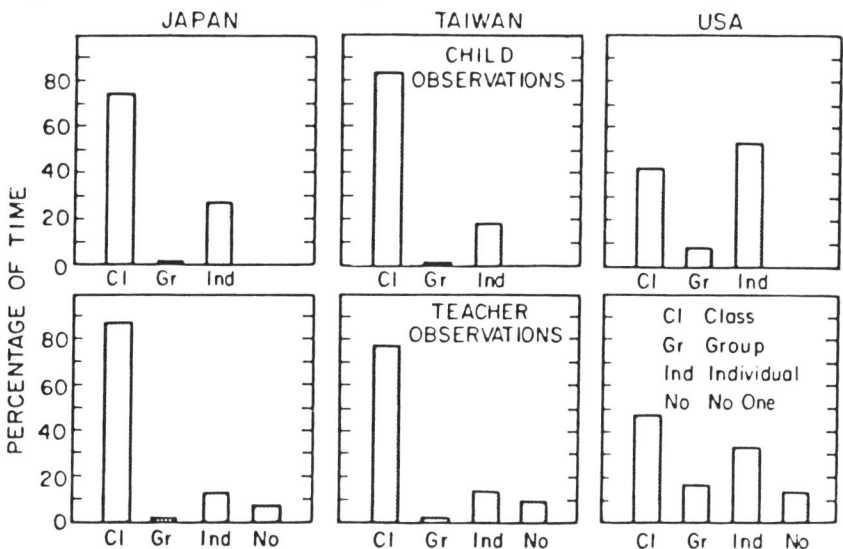

**Figure 2. Percentage of Time Spent in Various Classroom Organizations**

JAPAN — TAIWAN — USA
CHILD OBSERVATIONS
TEACHER OBSERVATIONS

Cl  Class
Gr  Group
Ind Individual
No  No One

*Source:* Stigler, Lee, and Stevenson, 1987.

class. The same picture emerges when teachers are observed (the lower panel of Figure 2). American teachers spent more time working with individuals and less time working with the whole class than did Chinese or Japanese teachers. In addition, American teachers were coded as working with no students 13 percent of the total time in mathematics classes, as opposed to only 6 percent of the time for Japanese teachers and 9 percent of the time for Chinese teachers.

The counterpart of these findings is displayed in Figure 3, where we see what percentage of the total time in mathematics classes students were part of a teacher-led activity and what percentage they were part of an activity with no leader. In Taiwan the teacher was the leader of the children's activities 90 percent of the time, as opposed to 74 percent in Japan and only 46 percent in the United States. No one was leading the students' activity 9 percent of the time in Taiwan, 26 percent of time in Japan, and 51 percent of the time in the United States.

Taken together, these findings indicate that classrooms in the Asian cultures are organized more hierarchically than are classrooms in the United States, with the teacher directing energies to the whole class and with students more often working under the direct supervision of the teacher. Because of these differences in organization, American students experience being taught by the teacher a much smaller percentage of time than do the Asian students, even though American classes contain roughly half the number of students.

**Figure 3. Percentage of Time Students Spent in Activity Led by Teacher and by No One**

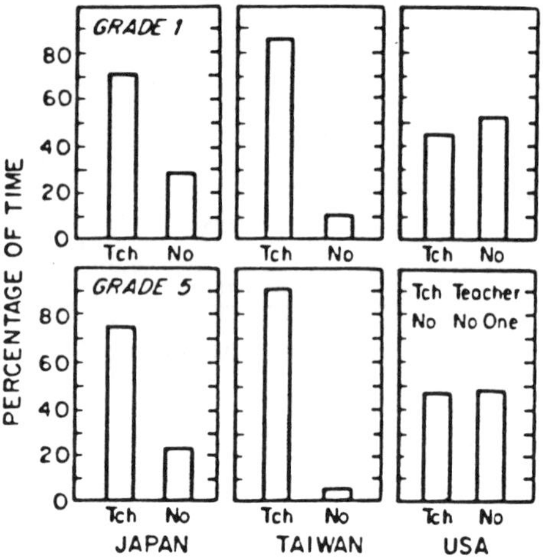

[Figure: Bar charts showing percentage of time for Grade 1 and Grade 5 in Japan, Taiwan, and USA, comparing Teacher-led (Tch) vs No One (No) activities]

*Source:* Stigler, Lee, and Stevenson, 1987.

Associated with the relatively decentralized organization that characterizes American classrooms is a higher level of disorderly behavior. This disorderliness was revealed in our coding of the incidence of inappropriate or off-task student behaviors. If the target child was not doing what the teacher expected him or her to do, he or she was judged as being off-task. Two categories of off-task were distinguished: those behaviors involving inappropriate peer interaction and those the target child engaged in alone. In addition we coded whether or not the target child was out of his or her seat. The results from these observations are presented in Figure 4.

There were large cross-cultural differences in the overall percentage of time students spent engaged in inappropriate, off-task activities. Across both grade levels, American students were off-task 17 percent of the time during mathematics class, as opposed to only 10 percent of the time for Chinese and Japanese students. Unfortunately, we did not code what students were actually doing but only that they were not behaving in accordance with classroom norms as defined by the teacher. Thus, we do not know whether some of the behavior coded as off-task might nevertheless have been oriented toward academic goals.

American students were coded as being out of their seats during mathematics classes 21 percent of the time, whereas Chinese and Japanese children were out of their seats 4 percent and 2 percent of the time, respectively. Of course, being out of one's seat does not necessarily imply that one is off-task, particularly in American classrooms. However, if we look at the percentage of time students were both out of their seats and

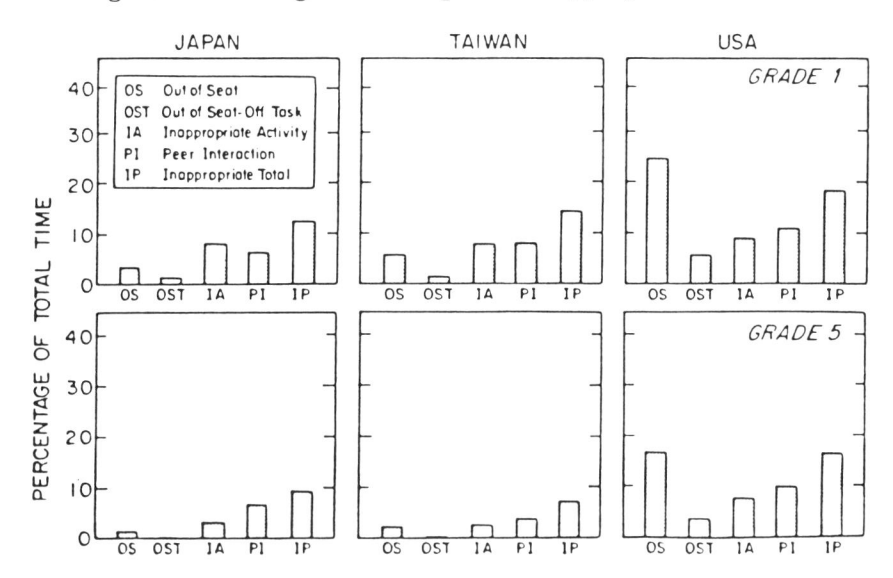

**Figure 4. Percentage of Time Spent in Inappropriate Activities**

|    |                        |
|----|------------------------|
| OS | Out of Seat            |
| OST| Out of Seat-Off Task   |
| IA | Inappropriate Activity |
| PI | Peer Interaction       |
| IP | Inappropriate Total    |

*Source:* Stigler, Lee, and Stevenson, 1987.

off-task, the American percentage was five times as high as that in the other two countries (5 percent versus less than 1 percent in Japan and Taiwan).

## Problem Solving, Evaluation, and Coherence: Preliminary Ideas from the Narrative Observations

The data derived from the first observational study is informative, up to a point: we get basic information about how time is spent by students in the three countries and about how frequently classrooms are organized in various ways. The limitation of these data is that we learn very little about how mathematics is actually taught in the three cultures. In contrast, the narrative observations collected in the current study provide us with richly detailed information concerning what happens in mathematics classes in Sendai, Taipei, and Chicago. In the remainder of this chapter we will present some ideas based on preliminary analyses of the narrative records.

Three ways in which classrooms in the three cultures were observed to vary were in the nature of mathematical problem-solving activities, the methods by which student work was evaluated, and the coherence of lessons from the child's point of view.

***Problem Solving.*** A major component of mathematics lessons in all three cultures involves learning how to solve, and then solving, mathematical problems. However, the styles of learning and instruction that surround problem solving, as well as the formats in which problems are presented, appear to differ greatly across cultures.

*Reflection Versus Performance.* In terms of style, classrooms vary in the degree to which they emphasize performance and practice, on the one hand, versus reflective thinking and verbalization, on the other. Chinese classrooms differ from Japanese classrooms in this regard: the Chinese classrooms are more performance oriented and the Japanese classrooms more reflective. American classrooms are not at all reflective, as are Japanese classrooms, nor do they place a consistent emphasis on performance, as do Chinese classrooms.

One index of reflectivity is simply the amount of verbal explanation, both by teachers and by students, that occurs during mathematics lessons. The percentages of segments that contained verbal explanations by the teacher, a student, or both are presented in Figure 5. In the first grade, 47 percent of all Japanese segments contained verbal explanations, compared to 21 percent of Chinese segments and 20 percent of American segments. By fifth grade, the incidence of explanations in classrooms in Taipei and Chicago has increased to 47 percent and 38 percent, respectively, but the incidence of explanations has increased in the Japanese segments as well, up to 51 percent. Clearly, there is more verbal discussion of mathematical concepts and procedures in Japanese classrooms than there is in either Chinese or American classrooms, and this difference is most pronounced in the first grade.

Indeed, when visiting a Japanese mathematics class, one detects a more relaxed pace than occurs in either Chinese or American classrooms. Japanese teachers tell students it is the process of problem solving that matters, not simply getting the correct answer. Japanese teachers thus often try to slow their students down, asking them to think about a problem and how to solve it, then discuss their thoughts with the class, rather than rushing on to solve the problem. Interestingly, Japanese fifth-grade teachers asked their students not to solve but to think about a problem in 7 percent of all segments, something that occurred in only 2 percent of the Chinese and American segments.

Chinese teachers, on the other hand, emphasize fast and accurate performance, or getting the right answer quickly. For example, 17 percent of all Chinese segments were devoted to practicing rapid mental calculation, an activity that was never observed in either the Japanese or American classrooms. It appears that Chinese teachers emphasize "do," the Japanese teachers emphasize "think."

*Manipulatives and Real-World Scenarios.* One might expect that the Japanese emphasis on reflection and verbalization would imply less reliance on concrete manipulatives or real-world problems. In fact, however, this was not the case. Both Japanese and Chinese teachers, as we

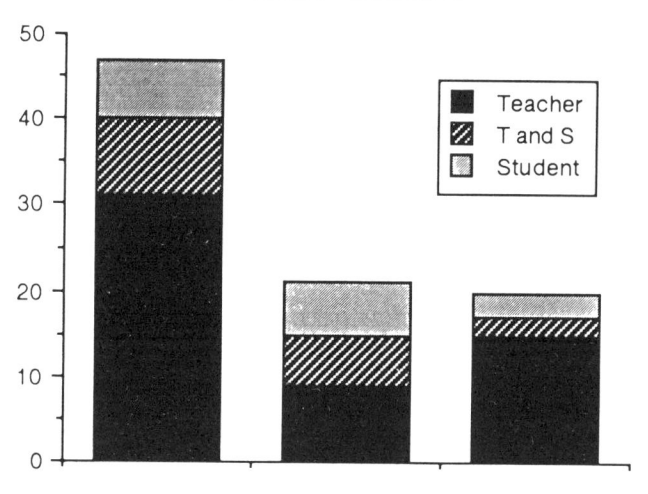

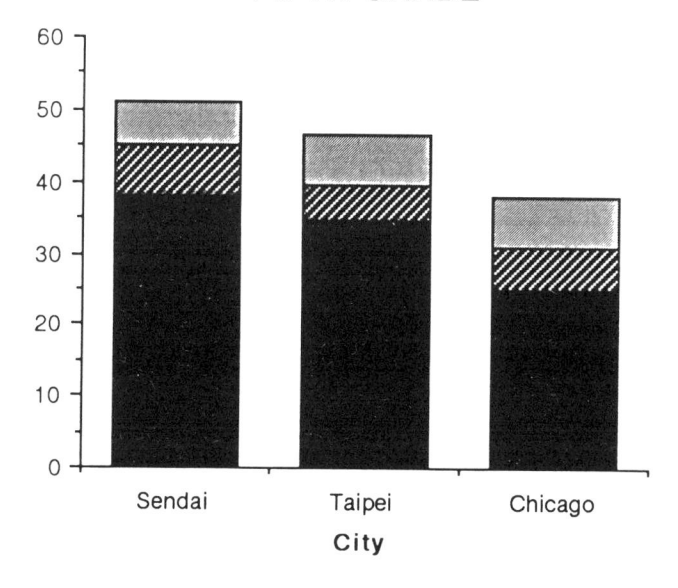

Figure 5. Percentage of Segments with Explanations from Teachers Only, from Students Only, and from Both Teachers and Students

will show, relied more on manipulatives and real-world problem situations than did teachers in our Chicago sample.

The use of concrete and real-world materials during classroom instruction was coded in two categories: (1) concrete manipulatives (for example, presented with eighty discrete objects, children are asked to divide them into four equal groups) and (2) real-world scenarios, which included word problems, dramatic enactments of mathematically solvable real-world problems, or the (relatively infrequent) situation where students are asked to generate a word problem to correspond with a symbolic equation. We assume that segments in which neither manipulatives nor real-world problems were used depended primarily on symbolic mathematical materials for instruction.

The percentages of instructional segments in which problems were presented using concrete manipulatives, real-world scenarios, or both are presented in Figure 6. The upper panel of Figure 6 shows that in first grade, both manipulatives and real-world scenarios are used more frequently in Taipei than in either Sendai or Chicago and more frequently in Sendai than in Chicago. In the fifth grade (lower panel of Figure 6), teachers in all three cultures have increased their use of real-world scenarios while at the same time reducing their reliance on manipulatives. However, there still are large differences between the three cultures on both counts: Sendai shows the largest proportion of segments in which real-world scenarios are used, and Chicago shows the least. Taipei teachers, on the other hand, use more manipulatives in fifth grade than do teachers in the other two locations, whereas Chicago teachers use the least. Thus, although Japanese and Chinese teachers differ in the degree to which they use manipulatives versus real-world content in their teaching of problem solving, both groups of Asian teachers use far more manipulatives and real-world problems combined than do the American teachers.

Children learn not only from the way that problems are presented but also from the type of feedback they receive and the manner in which that feedback is provided. Children are also sensitive to the ways that lessons are structured. Thus, two additional factors that seem to distinguish mathematics classrooms in Japan, Taiwan, and the United States are (1) the way in which feedback is provided to students, and (2) the degree to which students are provided with opportunities to construct coherent representations of mathematics lessons.

***Evaluation.*** Students' work is evaluated frequently in classrooms. We have found that both the frequency of and the approach to evaluations of students' mathematical solutions differ in the three cities.

Our first analysis reveals the frequency with which children's work is evaluated in the three cities. In first-grade mathematics lessons, 7 percent of all segments in Chicago were devoted to evaluation, whereas 12 percent

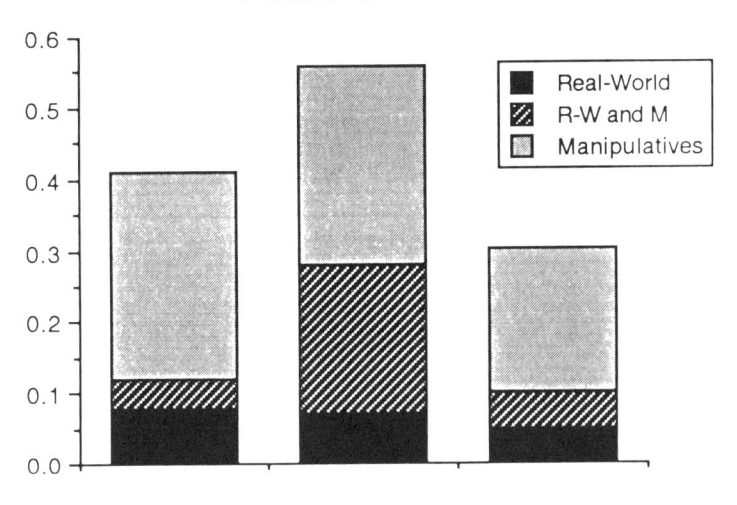

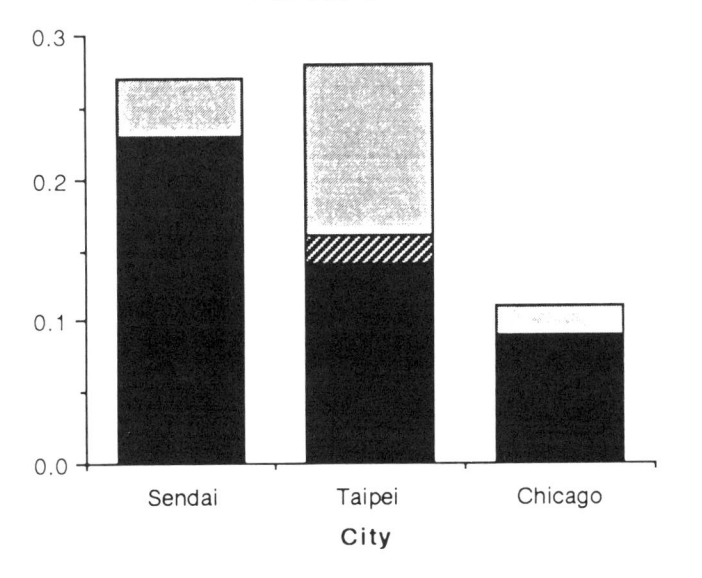

Figure 6. Proportion of Instructional Segments Using Concrete Manipulations, Real-World Scenarios, or Both

of segments in Sendai and 13 percent in Taipei were devoted to evaluation. Although evaluation segments occurred more often in fifth grade than in first grade, there were fewer such segments in the fifth grade in Chicago (14 percent) than in Sendai (17 percent) or Taipei (18 percent). Furthermore, although the evaluation that occurs in lesson segments devoted to evaluation is usually public and visible to the whole class, this was less true in Chicago than it was in Sendai or Taipei. Thus, students in Chicago have somewhat less opportunity to have their own work evaluated, and to observe the evaluation of other students' performance, than do students in the two Asian cities.

In addition to the differences in frequency of evaluation, we also have discovered differences in the methods used for evaluating students' work. Each evaluation segment was coded for how the students' answers were treated. In analyses of segments in which evaluation was the primary activity, the three most common methods of evaluation were as follows: (1) displaying a student's erroneous solution and reworking the problem until a correct solution was derived, (2) having students report to the class how many problems in a set of problems were solved correctly (for example, the teacher asks all students who solved all problems correctly to stand up), and (3) praising or rewarding students for their efforts and/or correct solutions. Not all evaluation segments used one of these three methods, but a sizable percentage did. Figure 7 presents the percentage of public evaluation segments in each country and grade level that employed each of the three methods. (It was only possible to code public evaluation segments, since only public evaluation was visible.)

It is clear from Figure 7 that the predominant methods for evaluating students differ for the students in the three cities and also differ from the first to the fifth grade. First-grade Japanese students are frequently evaluated by having their errors displayed to the class. These errors are then discussed, and correct solutions are derived by class members. This type of evaluation occurs in 35 percent of all first-grade evaluation segments in Sendai but in only 17 percent of the Taipei and 19 percent of the Chicago first-grade evaluation segments. The most prevalent type of evaluation in Taipei was reporting to the class the number of problems correctly solved. This occurs in 28 percent of the Sendai, 33 percent of the Taipei, and 23 percent of the Chicago first-grade evaluations. The most prevalent type of evaluation found in the Chicago first-grade segments was praising students. Thus, in the first grade, the Japanese students are revising their incorrect attempts, the Chinese students are letting the class know how well they performed, and the American students are being told that they have done a good job.

The picture changes somewhat when we examine the evaluations that occur in the fifth grade. Fifth-grade students in Taipei are often evaluated by having their errors displayed to their classmates (in 24 per-

**Figure 7.** Percentage of Evaluation Segments Containing Different Kinds of Feedback

*FIRST GRADE*

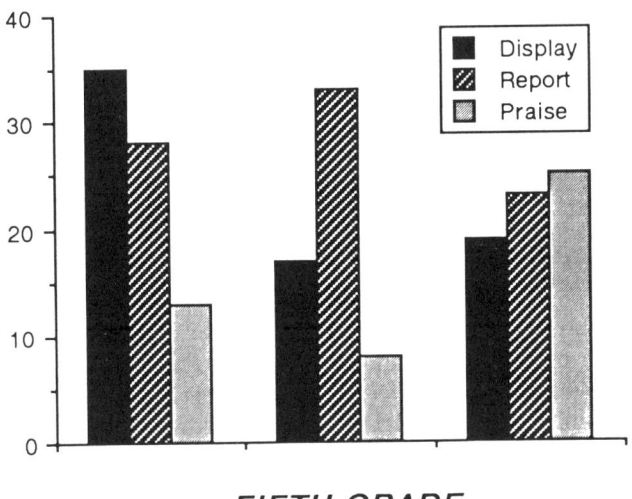

*FIFTH GRADE*

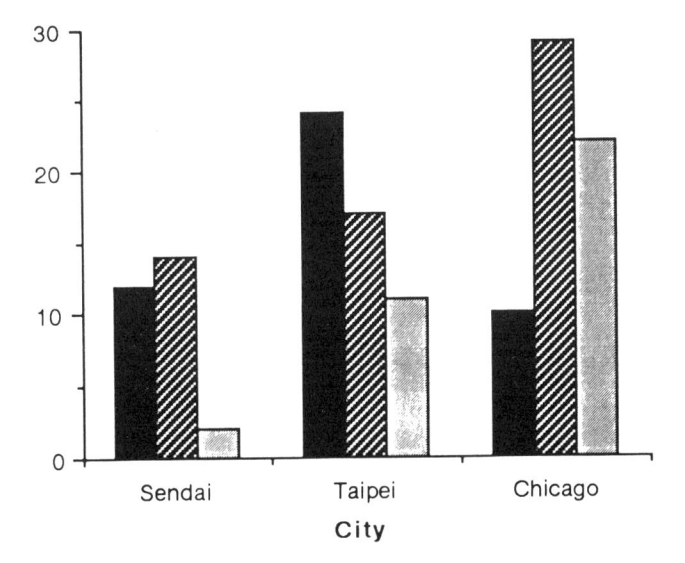

City

cent of the evaluation segments), whereas this happens less frequently in Sendai (in only 12 percent of the evaluation segments) and in Chicago (in only 10 percent of the evaluation segments). The fifth-grade students in Chicago and in Sendai are evaluated most frequently by announcing how many problems they solved correctly. However, this happens much more in Chicago (in 29 percent of the evaluation segments) than in either Sendai (in 14 percent of the evaluation segments) or in Taipei (in 17 percent of the evaluation segments). And finally, students in Chicago are still receiving more praise (22 percent of the evaluation segments) than are students in either Sendai (2 percent) or Taipei (11 percent).

*Coherence.* This last dimension is also the most speculative and difficult to document. Having read the corpus of narrative observations, we are left with the impression that Japanese classrooms in particular, and Chinese classrooms to some extent, are structured in a more coherent fashion than are American classrooms. We use the word *coherent* very much in the way researchers studying text comprehension use the word. A text is coherent to the extent that it enables or allows the comprehender to infer relations between events (Trabasso and van den Broek, 1985). In like manner, teachers who provide a basis for children to infer reasons for and relations between events provide the basis for coherence in the classroom. Work by Trabasso, Stein, and others has shown that coherence across events in a story has a profound impact on the ease with which the reader can encode, understand, and remember the events of a story (Trabasso and van den Broek, 1985; Stein and Policastro, 1984). Our speculation is that mathematics lessons, too, may be easier to comprehend, and students likely to learn more, when the episodes that comprise the class are coherent.

The analogy between a story and a mathematics classroom is not perfect, but it is close enough to be useful for thinking about the process by which children might construct meaning from their experiences in mathematics class. A mathematics class, like a story, consists of sequences of events related to each other and, hopefully, to the goals of the lesson. What we tend to find in the American observations, unfortunately, are sequences of events that go together, much like those in an ill-formed story. If it is difficult for adult observers to construct a coherent representation of the events that constitute a first- or fifth-grade mathematics class, then it surely would be even more difficult for the average child sitting in those classes to do so.

What, specifically, do we see in Asian classrooms that lead us to perceive them as being more coherent? One possibility is the small amount of time, relative to American classrooms, that is spent on transitions from one activity to another and on irrelevant interruptions. In American first-grade classrooms, a total of 21 percent of all segments contain transitions or irrelevant interruptions, compared to 7 percent in Sendai and

14 percent in Taipei. In fifth grade the corresponding percentages are 15 percent, 3 percent, and 3 percent. Rarely is the logical flow of an Asian class broken to pursue less mathematically important business (such as the time-consuming distribution of materials) that may give students the wrong idea about what is important about mathematics.

Another aspect of Asian classrooms that may facilitate coherence is a tendency we observed both in Japan and Taiwan to devote an entire forty-minute mathematics class to the solution of only one or two problems. In such a lesson, students might discuss the features of the problem, solve the problem using alternative methods, discuss and evaluate the alternative solution strategies, model the problem using manipulatives, and so on. The problem thus serves to provide topical continuity across the different segments of a lesson, much as a protagonist's goals and purposes provide continuity across the events of a story.

Assuming that a lesson with fewer problems is more coherent than one with more problems, it is worthwhile to ask whether there is, in fact, a large difference in number of problems presented across Japanese, Chinese, and American mathematics lessons. In a preliminary analysis, we counted the number of problems presented during fifth-grade instructional segments that lasted five minutes (the median length of all fifth-grade segments with ongoing instruction). The distribution of five-minute segments over number of problems presented is shown in Figure 8. What we find is that 75 percent of all five-minute instructional segments in Sendai focused on only one problem, compared to 55 percent of the segments in Taipei and only 17 percent of the segments in Chicago.

The devotion of even five minutes to a single problem was relatively rare in American classrooms, not to mention spending an entire class period on only one problem. In no class did we observe an American teacher sticking with a single problem for an entire class. Indeed it appears that American teachers value just the opposite approach. In recent research that examined characteristics of expert mathematics teachers in the United States, it was reported that the expert elementary mathematics teacher can get through forty problems in a single class, whereas the novice teacher may only cover six or seven problems (Leinhardt, 1986; Leinhardt and Greeno, 1986). It would appear that the Japanese or Chinese teacher is striving for a different goal. Or perhaps they are just adapting to a different reality: The value placed on homework in both of these Asian cultures means that repetitive practice can be accomplished at home and class can be reserved for teaching. American teachers must, especially at the first-grade level, accomplish both purposes during the school day.

It is important to note that sticking to one problem does not imply a boring class that lacks variety. Variety, as indexed by change in segment, is approximately equal across the three cultures. For example, the typi-

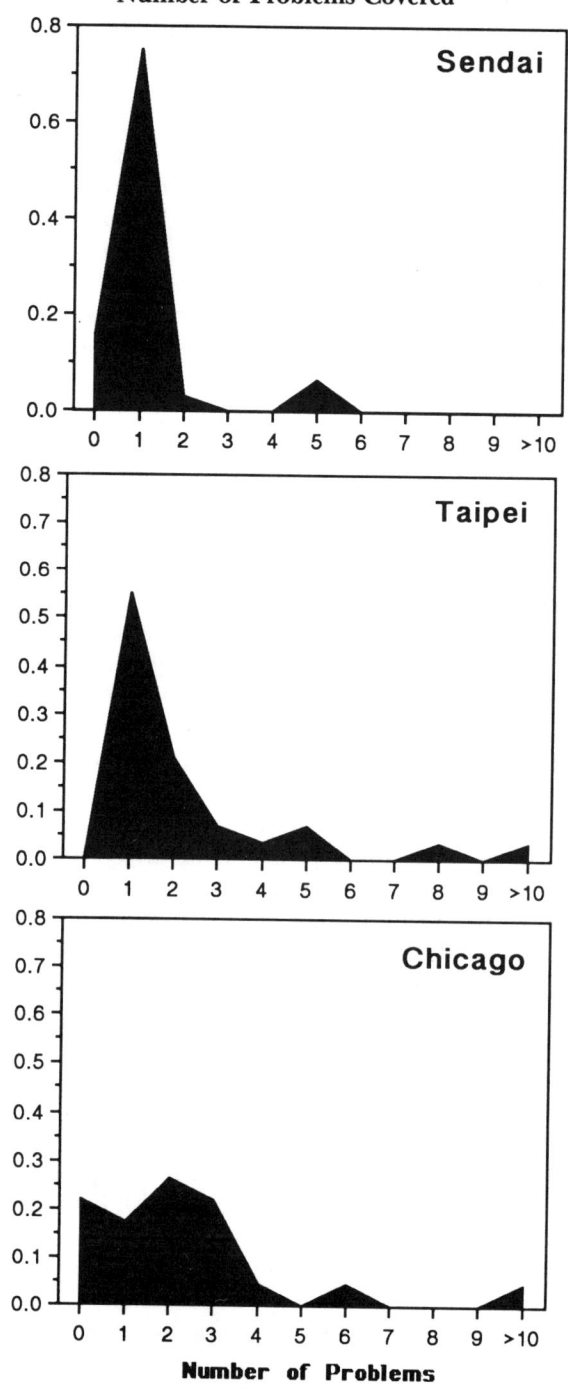

Figure 8. Distribution of Five-Minute Instructional Segments by Number of Problems Covered

cally first-grade mathematics class in all three cities consists of five or six segments, each lasting seven or eight minutes. What is different is the nature of the changes that occur from one segment to another. While in Japan and Taiwan segment changes are more often coded because of changes in materials or activities without a change in topic being taught, in American classrooms changes are more often coded because of a change in the topic being taught (also see Berliner and Tikunoff, 1976). In the first grade, changes in segments in Japan were due to a change in topic only 7 percent of the time, in Taiwan, 16 percent of the time, and in the United States, 25 percent of the time. This pattern is even more striking in the fifth grade: changes in segments in Japan were due to a change in topic only 1 percent of the time, in Taiwan, only 3 percent of the time, and in the United States, 17 percent of the time. Thus, the students in our Chicago sample must have had to change gears more frequently than their peers in Taipei and Sendai, within the bounds of a single mathematics lesson. And it is important to remember that changing topics does not mean merely a change in problem but rather a change on the order of starting with measurement and moving to multidigit addition. For example, one first-grade American class started with a segment on measurement, then proceeded to a segment on simple addition, then to a segment on telling time, and then to another segment on addition. The whole sequence was called "math class" by the teacher, but it is unclear how this sequence would have been interpreted by a child. In this case, it seems that it would be impossible for anyone to construct a coherent account of the whole class.

In other cases, where the topic does not change within a lesson, the sequence itself could be construed coherently, but American teachers do little to help the child construct a coherent representation. A good example of this kind of situation is provided by the topic of measurement as it is normally taught in first-grade classrooms. Most American textbooks teach fundamental measurement in the following sequence: First they teach children to compare quantities directly and to say which is longer, wider, and so on. Next, nonstandard units of measurement are introduced, and children are taught to ascertain, for example, how many paper clips long their pencils are. Finally, students are introduced to the concept of standard units and taught to measure objects in inches or centimeters. This is a sensible sequence and could conceivably be taught in a coherent manner.

Let us examine the way in which this sequence is implemented in one American classroom in our sample. In the first segment, the teacher has children examine objects—pencils, crayons, paperclips, chalk, and so on—and compare them to determine which are longer. The teacher then moves the class to the next segment and says:

OK, open your workbooks to page 12. I want you to measure your desk in pencils, find out how many pencils it takes to go across your desk, and write the answer on the line in your workbooks. [Children carry out instructions.] Ok, the next line says to use green crayons, but we don't have green crayons so we are going to use blue crayons. Raise your hand if you don't have a blue crayon. [Teacher takes approximately 10 minutes to pass out blue crayons to students who raise their hands; coded as a transition segment.] Now write the number of blue crayons next to the line that says green crayons. [Teacher then moves on to the third segment.] OK, now take out your centimeter ruler and measure the number of centimeters across your desk and write the number on the line in your workbooks.

What is fascinating about this particular class is that there is absolutely no marking by the teacher of the transition points—the three segments just follow each other as though there were no transition. There is no discussion of how each exercise is important in providing students with an understanding of measurement, no discussion of why units are important or why standard units are important, no discussion of historical development of measurement procedures that could provide more meaning to the sequence of activities, and no discussion of the goals of the class and how each activity relates to those goals. More time is devoted to making sure students have a blue crayon—which is totally irrelevant to the purpose of the lesson—than to conveying the purpose of the three segments on measurement. If we put ourselves in the child's position, what is the likelihood that we would construct a coherent, meaningful account of this particular class?

In Chinese classrooms, and in Japanese classrooms to an even greater extent, we see teachers explicitly pointing out to children the relationships that obtain between different segments within a lesson and between different lessons. For example, one Japanese first-grade teacher was quoted as asking this question of a student at the beginning of a mathematics class. "Would you explain the difference between what we learned in the previous lesson and what you came across in preparing for today's lesson?" To hear a question of this sort posed to a six-year-old would be surprising to most American educators. Perhaps more surprising is that the student was able to answer the question.

As another example, a teacher might draw parallels between a problem solved symbolically and the same problem solved with concrete manipulatives. In both of these examples, the students are given the opportunity to infer coherence across the episodes that constitute their experience in mathematics class. Transitions in the Asian classes often are marked by verbal discussion of the relation between two segments, and classes, especially in Japan, often start with the teacher explaining the goal of the day's class and how the activities relate to the goal. In our narrative data, we found that the Japanese teachers were twice as likely to make explicit reference to connections across episodes than were either the Chinese or American teachers (9 percent of all segments, compared to 5 percent and 4 percent).

In sum, the children we observed in our American sample are faced with a very difficult task: they are required to solve many problems on their own, and often there is no apparent link among the types of problems they are being asked to solve. This clearly differs from the way mathematics classes proceed in Taipei and Sendai. Although the Chinese and Japanese lessons were different on many dimensions, children in both of these cultures were given better opportunities to construct mathematical concepts and also were given more opportunities to get public feedback about whether their constructions were accurate.

## Conclusion

Japanese and Chinese elementary school students are learning more about all aspects of mathematics than are their peers in the United States. Although there are many possible explanations for these differences, we have chosen, in this chapter, to focus on classrooms, since classrooms are the context in which most children learn mathematics. What we have found is not surprising, given the cross-cultural differences in achievement: classrooms in Sendai and Taipei differ markedly from those in our American samples on a number of dimensions.

In our first study, which employed a time-sampling objective coding scheme, we found that students in both Sendai and Taipei spend a great deal more time in mathematics class than do American students and that they spend less time during mathematics class engaged in off-task, inappropriate behaviors. We also found that classrooms are organized differently in the Asian cultures. Whereas Asian students spend most of their time working on teacher-led activities as members of a whole class of students, American students spend more time working independently, with contact with the teacher more likely to take the form of individualized or small-group instruction. These differences in organization mean that American students spend much less time in school being attended to by the teacher, if we assume that students working as members of a whole class feel that the teacher is working with them.

Why do we organize our U.S. mathematics classes in the way that we do? Some part of the answer can be tied to cultural beliefs about the nature of individual differences and the nature of learning. In other research conducted by the Michigan group, we have found that American mothers are more likely to see mathematical ability as innately determined than are Asian mothers (Stevenson, Lee, and Stigler, 1986).

Because we tend to think individual children are inherently unique in their limitations, we believe that the education appropriate for one child may not be appropriate for another, and thus we tend to emphasize individualized learning. Asian educators are more comfortable in the belief that all children, with proper effort, can take advantage of a uniform educational experience, and so they are able to focus on providing the same, high-quality experience to all students. Our results suggest that American educators need to question their long-held assumption that an individualized learning experience is inherently a higher-quality, more effective experience than is a whole-class learning experience. Although it may be true that an equal amount of time with a teacher may be more effective in a one-on-one situation than in a large-group situation, we must realize that the result of individualized instruction given realistic financial constraints is to drastically reduce the amount of time a teacher can spend with any individual student.

In our narrative observations, preliminary analyses again revealed a number of differences in the way mathematics is taught in Asian and American classrooms. Asian students are given more opportunities for solving real-world problems, and Japanese students, in particular, spend a far greater amount of time than do either Chinese or American students engaging in reflective verbalization about mathematics. We also found a greater reliance on public evaluation of both the products and the processes of students' problem-solving efforts. In Japan the most common form of evaluation involved children putting their incorrect solutions on the blackboard for all to see and then having the whole class discuss the nature of the error and possible ways of correcting it.

This brings us back to the earlier story of the Japanese classroom. We can see that it represents quite well many of the characteristics of mathematics learning in Japanese classrooms: the whole class working together; talking but not off task; one child publicly displaying his failed solution, not to be ridiculed but rather to be corrected by his classmates. How is it possible for this scenario to occur so frequently in Japan but so little in the United States? The answer, again, lies in cultural differences. Not only are children in the United States rarely evaluated in this manner, but it is considered by many cruel to do so. If errors in mathematics are seen as due more to innate ability differences than to educable factors, then it would be regarded as cruel to publicly demonstrate a child's failings, which are no fault of his or her own. It may be that the costs of such a technique, within the context of American culture, outweigh the advantages that may derive from the analysis of incorrect problem solutions. For better or worse, American teachers feel more comfortable praising the student who performs well than discussing the errors that can occur in the course of problem solving. Unfortunately, praise is not a particularly good way to start a deep discussion of mathematics principles and procedures.

The most difficult questions, of course, remain unanswered. These are (1) which, if any, of the differences we have found cause the differences in performance? and (2) which aspects of Asian classrooms, if implemented in the context of American education, would contribute to enhancing the learning of American children? At present we cannot provide answers to these questions, and this kind of survey research will never be able to do so. What we hope to have done is to provide American educators with a picture of classroom learning that is different from our own and which thus may function to train attention back on assumptions about learning mathematics that are implicitly present in American mathematics classrooms. As White (1987) has pointed out, comparisons of education in Japan and the United States provide us not with a blueprint but rather with a mirror that can sharpen our awareness of how we educate our children and how we might do it differently. We hope that the research reported in this chapter will serve this purpose and will inspire the awareness and experimentation that will be required to understand how children in different cultures learn mathematics from classroom instruction.

**References**

Berliner, D. C., and Tikunoff, W. J. "The California Beginning Teacher Evaluation Study: Overview of the Ethnographic Study." *Journal of Teacher Education*, 1976, *27* (1), 24-30.

Husen, T. *International Study of Achievement in Mathematics*. New York: Wiley, 1967.

Leinhardt, G. "Expertise in Math Teaching." *Educational Leadership*, 1986, *43* (7), 28-33.

Leinhardt, G., and Greeno, J. G. "The Cognitive Skill of Teaching." *Journal of Educational Psychology*, 1986, *78* (2), 75-95.

McKnight, C. C., Crosswhite, F. J., Dossey, J. A., Kifer, E., Swafford, J. O., Travers, K. J., and Cooney, T. J. *The Underachieving Curriculum: Assessing U.S. School Mathematics from an International Perspective*. Champaign, Ill.: Stipes, 1987.

Spiro, M. E. "On the Strange and the Familiar in Recent Anthropological Thought." In J. Stigler, R. Shweder, and G. Herdt (eds.), *Culture and Human Development*. New York: Cambridge University Press, in press.

Stein, N. L., and Policastro, M. "The Concept of a Story: A Comparison Between Children's and Teachers' Perspectives." In H. Mandl, N. L. Stein, and T. Trabasso (eds.), *Learning and Comprehension of Text*. Hillsdale, N.J.: Erlbaum, 1984.

Stevenson, H. W., Lee, S. Y., and Stigler, J. W. "Mathematics Achievement of Chinese, Japanese, and American Children." *Science*, 1986, *231*, 693-699.

Stigler, J. W., Lee, S. Y., Lucker, G. W., and Stevenson, H. W. "Curriculum and Achievement in Mathematics: A Study of Elementary School Children in Japan, Taiwan, and the United States." *Journal of Educational Psychology*, 1982, *74* (3), 315-322.

Stigler, J. W., Lee, S. Y., and Stevenson, H. W. "Mathematics Classrooms in Japan, Taiwan, and the United States." *Child Development*, 1987, *58*, 1272-1285.

Trabasso, T., and van den Broek, P. "Causal Thinking at Story Comprehension." *Memory and Language,* 1985, *24,* 612–630.

Travers, K. J., Crosswhite, F. J., Dossey, J. A., Swafford, J. O., McKnight, C. C., and Cooney, T. J. *Second International Mathematics Study Summary Report for the United States.* Champaign, Ill.: Stipes, 1985.

Tukey, J. W. *Exploratory Data Analysis.* Reading, Mass.: Addison-Wesley, 1977.

White, M. *The Japanese Educational Challenge: A Commitment to Children.* New York: Free Press, 1987.

*James W. Stigler is assistant professor in the Departments of Behavioral Sciences and Education at the University of Chicago.*

*Michelle Perry is assistant professor of developmental psychology and of the combined program in education and psychology at the University of Michigan.*

*Encountering novel problems continuously, being encouraged to seek comprehension, freedom from urgent need for rewards, and dialogical interaction all aid mathematical understanding.*

# Social and Motivational Bases for Mathematical Understanding

*Giyoo Hatano*

### Distinguishing Between Adaptive and Routine Experts

The development of mathematical cognition is undoubtedly based on learners' experience, more specifically on practice in solving mathematical problems. It can be conceptualized as a process of acquiring expertise—that is, the accumulation and reorganization of domain-specific knowledge through problem solving. Recent studies on expert-novice differences in knowledge-rich domains such as physics and mathematics have shown that experts, using their rich and well-organized body of knowledge, generate an appropriate representation of a problem so that they can handle it easily to solve the problem (Chi, Glaser, and Rees, 1982; Glaser, 1986).

However, not all experts are flexible enough to be able to solve novel types of problems, even within the domain in which they have acquired expertise. While some learners are flexible in their use of those mathematical formulae and computation procedures they know, others can apply their problem-solving skills efficiently but only to the types of problems they have practiced routinely.

Hatano and Inagaki (1986) attribute this difference in flexibility or adaptiveness to the extent of conceptual knowledge possessed. People who are regarded as experts in the target domain have a body of procedural knowledge needed to solve familiar types of problems promptly. They have procedures for making judgments as well as executing actions. However, they may not have conceptual knowledge, which is defined here as "more or less comprehensive knowledge of the nature of the object" of the procedures. The object may be a physical entity, for example, a device people operate many times, a plant they raise, and so on. The knowledge about the entity is often called a mental model (Gentner and Stevens, 1983)—a set of properties of the object, which people can use in mental simulations. The object may also be a cognitive entity characterized by its rich relationships (Hiebert and Lefevre, 1986), such as the decimal system of numbers.

Because of conceptual knowledge, which enables one to find the meaning of each step of the procedure in terms of the object's properties and their changes, one can understand how and why a given procedure works. More specifically, one can explain why the procedure is valid—that is, one can obtain what Greeno (1980) calls explicit understanding. With conceptual knowledge one can also judge not only the conventional version but also variations of the procedure as appropriate or inappropriate and then modify the procedure according to changes in constraints—that is, one can achieve implicit understanding (Greeno, 1980). For example, the conceptual knowledge of the decimal number system is the basis for explaining the borrowing procedure, differentiating "buggy algorithms" from unusual but valid procedures, and applying flexibly the procedure of multidigit subtraction.

In this way, we distinguish adaptive experts—those who have acquired rich conceptual knowledge—from routine experts—those who have not acquired such knowledge. While the latter are also experts by virtue of their speed and accuracy in solving routine problems, they are not able to "invent" new procedures. All they can do when given a novel type of problem or an apparently familiar one under modified conditions is to make minor adjustments, relying on trial and error.

Two comments are added to avoid possible misinterpretations: First, the skills of routine experts—applying procedures without conceptual knowledge—are not useless. To be a competent problem solver, one has to know how to apply the procedure and when to do so, but one does not have to go beyond this. We can solve a great number of mathematical problems using the right procedure at the right time without having the corresponding conceptual knowledge or understanding based on it. Very few of us in fact can explain why a given procedure (for instance, "To divide fractions, reverse the numerator and denominator of the divisor and multiply") works, though we believe it is valid and we can apply it efficiently. Lack of conceptual knowledge becomes a serious deficit only when unusual, novel types of problems are posed. Thus, after having applied a procedure many times successfully, we may lose interest in knowing why the procedure works, because we take it for granted.

Second, conceptual knowledge may be incomplete or incorrect. A person may know that an orchid is similar to a cactus without being able to specify the differences between the two. Conceptual knowledge may involve false elements, as revealed most clearly in the case of so-called misconceptions, which contradict some known facts yet explain others. For example, many children believe that a potted plant can grow if it is given only water.

### How and When Is Conceptual Knowledge Acquired?

No one has proposed a well-articulated theory, but typically conceptual knowledge is acquired by the process of constructing, elaborating, or revising the model so that it will plausibly explain a set of observed relationships. This process accompanies abduction, that is, the constrained generation of explanatory hypotheses based on limited data.

Consider an example of this process of abduction and of the construction of a model. After accumulated experience of growing flowers, a five-year-old girl stated, "Flowers are like people. If flowers eat nothing, they will fall down of hunger. If they eat too much, they will be taken ill" (Motoyoshi, 1979). The child generated explanations for her observations—that is, either giving no water or too much water makes flowers wither—by personifying flowers. In this process, she has developed a model of flowers as having a human-like structure. She chose this explanation from among a great many possible explanations, probably because her induction was constrained by the tendency to transfer knowledge about humans to all other living things, which is common among young children (Carey, 1985; Hatano and Inagaki, 1987a).

When is conceptual knowledge likely to be acquired? It is assumed that conceptual knowledge cannot be transmitted verbally or graphically. In other words, it must be constructed by each individual, though the process of construction can be guided to some extent by direct or indirect teaching. Its construction—formation, elaboration, or revision—is likely to occur, often as a by-product, when one seeks causal explanations for a given set of observed connections (for example, why a given procedure produces particular results). One is seldom engaged in activities aiming at the construction per se, though once constructed, conceptual knowledge plays an important role in solving various types of novel problems.

### A Model of Adaptive Expertise

Under what circumstances does one construct rich conceptual knowledge and become an adaptive expert? What conditions tend to lead one to a routine expert, even after applying procedures many times to solve a large number of problems in a given domain?

How likely one is to acquire conceptual knowledge depends on the nature of the object and procedures for dealing with it. Among others, the following two cognitive conditions seem critical: (1) more or less appropriate models of the object can easily be obtained, and (2) steps of the procedures can easily be separated and manipulated. Since this acquisition is a process of building a model and checking it with the data, a good candidate model, even if very tentative and implicit, must be available. Knowledge may be obtained primarily through perception, as a somewhat vague image of the object (for example, we can learn how a water-drinking doll works by breaking it up and observing its parts closely), and by verbal and graphic description of the object's major characteristics (for example, a blueprint of a machine helps us understand it). Or knowledge may be derived indirectly on the basis of its functions or reactions. In the latter case, it is usually borrowed from elsewhere, as in the above example of personification of flowers. Knowledge acquisition also required multiple observations in which the procedure is broken down into steps or components and some are varied more or less systematically. In order to check a hypothetically assigned meaning, one has to change or omit the critical step or component. Such system observation, most evident among scientists, is needed to some extent in acquiring conceptual knowledge.

Although these two cognitive conditions are necessary, they are far from sufficient for the acquisition of conceptual knowledge and adaptive expertise. It is difficult to explain why very few students become adaptive experts in terms of cognitive conditions alone. In addition to cognitive conditions, motivational conditions seem critical. Assuming cognitive conditions are satisfied, one is likely to become an adaptive expert if and only if he or she is motivated to understand why procedures work while using them for problem solving.

***When Are We Motivated to Understand?*** My colleague and I (Hatano and Inagaki, 1987b) have tried to formulate a process model of the arousal of motivation for comprehension drawing on Berlyne's theory of epistemic behavior (Berlyne, 1963, 1965a, 1965b). This theory assumes that, since human beings are intrinsically motivated to understand the world, "cognitive incongruity"—that is, a state where a person feels that his or her comprehension is intolerably inadequate—motivates a person to pursue subjectively adequate comprehension or satisfactory explanations. Cognitive incongruity induces enduring comprehension activity, including seeking further information from the outside, retrieving another piece of prior knowledge, generating new inferences, examining the compatibility of inferences more closely, and so on.

Three types of cognitive incongruity are distinguished. One is surprise, which is induced when a person encounters an event or information that disconfirms a prediction based on prior knowledge. A person will be motivated to understand why the prediction has failed and how to repair the prior knowledge by incorporating the new information. Another is perplexity, which is induced when a person is aware of equally plausible but competing ideas (predictions, assertions, explanations, and so forth) related to the target object or procedure. In this case one seeks further information in order not only to choose one of the alternatives but also to find justifications for the choice. The third is discoordination. This is the awareness of a lack of coordination among some or all of the pieces of knowledge involved. In other words, it is induced when one recognizes that though pieces of knowledge about the target are available, they are not well connected or that other pieces of related information cannot be generated by combining or in any way transforming the existing ones.

It should be noted, however, that the objective lack or inadequacy of comprehension does not always induce cognitive incongruity, nor does cognitive incongruity always induce comprehension activity. In order for cognitive incongruity to occur, people must themselves recognize the inadequacy of their comprehension. To do this, they must be able to monitor their own comprehension.

There exist two limiting conditions to be fulfilled before cognitive incongruity leads to enduring comprehension activity. One limiting condition is that people realize the importance and possibility of comprehension. Only when people have confidence in their ability to understand and when they experience cognitive incongruity about a target they value (because it is relevant to their lives) are they likely to engage in comprehension activity. Otherwise, they will be reluctant to engage in comprehension activity (which requires much mental effort), and they may suppress the motivation to comprehend.

The other limiting condition is the freedom from any urgent external need—for material reward, positive evaluation, or definitely correct answers. Studies on the so-called undermining effects of extrinsic rewards have shown that promised or given rewards deteriorate both the quality of performance in the task and intrinsic interest (Lepper, 1983; Lepper and Greene, 1978). This suggests, though indirectly, the possibility that extrinsic rewards inhibit motivation for comprehension. The expectation of rewards may change the goal of ongoing cognitive activity from comprehension to obtaining such rewards (Inagaki, 1980).

From the process model described so far, we can deduce the following three conditions under which a student is likely to be motivated to comprehend procedures used for problem solving and thus to become an adaptive expert in a domain:

1. *One encounters novel types of problems continuously in the course*

*of acquiring expertise.* Whereas familiar types of problems can easily be solved by applying the known procedure in an algorithmic way, thus avoiding cognitive incongruity, novel types of problems tend to produce perplexity and discoordination. Finding that a proposed solution is wrong tends to induce surprise.

2. *One is encouraged to seek comprehension.* Encouragement of comprehension leads an individual to form metacognitive beliefs emphasizing the significance and capability of comprehension (at least in the domain in which expertise is acquired); this makes comprehension activity likely to occur when cognitive incongruity is induced.

3. *One is free from urgent need to obtain external reinforcement when solving problems.* One can pursue comprehension only when the pressure to obtain rewards is not very strong, because engaging in comprehension activity is seldom the surest and shortest way to rewards. When solving a problem correctly is vitally important, one is likely to concentrate on it, suppressing cognitive incongruity.

The process model described above implies that the arousal of motivation for comprehension depends heavily on prior knowledge. In order for incongruity to be induced, one has to have relevant pieces of well-established knowledge. Surprise is felt only after a firm expectation is derived from prior knowledge. Perplexity is induced when more alternatives than one are judged plausible in the light of prior knowledge. Discoordination may occur only when a fair amount of relevant knowledge is available for further processing. Furthermore, as suggested by Markman (1981), people can promptly recognize the inadequacy of comprehension only in the domains where they have acquired rich and well-structured knowledge—that is, in their "domains of expertise." Likewise, individuals have their own "domains of interest" in which they believe they are able to comprehend and also in which the comprehension is valuable and independent of external rewards. People are willing to engage in prolonged comprehension activity in these domains.

However, outside their domains of expertise and interest, people are unlikely to recognize the inadequacy of their comprehension, unlikely to engage in comprehension activity even when incongruity is aroused, and, as a consequence, unlikely to acquire knowledge through comprehension. This vicious cycle of people as cognitive systems cannot be broken by introducing external reinforcement, because people are likely to be attracted to seek it, moving further away from comprehension.

***Dialogical Interaction Induces Comprehension Activity.*** Those activities that can amplify motivation for comprehension outside the domains of expertise and interest are social-interactional ones in most cases. Dialogical interactions, such as discussion, controversy, and reciprocal teaching, in which knowledge or comprehension is to be shared often serve to enhance comprehension activity. Miyake (1986) poses a good example of how dialogical interaction motivates persons to engage in prolonged comprehension activity that would not be induced without a partner. When asked to find why a sewing machine can make stitches, Miyake found that pairs of subjects spent as long as sixty to ninety minutes trying to integrate different perspectives and knowledge bases through discussion. One of the pair claimed to understand the device before long, but criticism by the partner created once again the state of nonunderstanding (cognitive incongruity) that motivated the pursuit of deeper levels of understanding.

Why is dialogical interaction effective in inducing comprehension activity even among those students who lack rich and well-organized knowledge? Such interaction (1) tends to produce and amplify surprise, perplexity, and discoordination by helping people monitor their comprehension; and (2) relates the less familiar domain to one's domains of expertise and interest.

Surprise can be aroused by asking a person to make a prediction and then giving information that clearly disconfirms it. Surprise can be heightened when the prediction is given openly and unmistakably in dialogue. Perplexity is induced when one finds different ideas among fellow participants in dialogical interaction. The presence of others expressing different ideas is especially advantageous for amplifying perplexity, because one has to confront them. It is harder to maintain as plausible those ideas one merely reads or is exposed to passively.

A person may experience discoordination in the process of trying to explain why his or her views are reasonable when asked for clarification or when the views are directly challenged or disputed. Why is discoordination induced in such situations? Inagaki (1986) offers three reasons: First, one has to verbalize (make explicit what has been known only implicitly) in the process of trying to convince or teach others. This will lead one to examine one's own comprehension in detail and thus become aware of any thus far unnoticed inadequacies in the coordination among those pieces of knowledge. Second, since persuasion or teaching requires the orderly presentation of ideas, one has to organize better intra-individually what has been known. Third, for effective argumentation or teaching, one must incorporate opposing ideas—that is, coordinate different points of view inter-individually between proponents and opponents or between tutors and learners. Strong discoordination occurs only when one struggles to coordinate, since it is practically impossible to coordinate all the pieces of information available at any given moment.

Discussion, controversy, or teaching satisfies the first limiting condition as well—that is, it can help one realize the importance and possibility of comprehension. First, any of these elements invites a person to "commit" to some ideas by requiring the person to state the ideas to others, thereby placing the issue in question in the domains of interest.

Second, the social setting makes the enterprise of comprehension meaningful. Unless extrinsic motivation (such as winning the debate) is so strong that is supercedes motivation for comprehension, this social aspect will make comprehension activity enduring.

The above discussion strongly suggests that dialogical interaction enhances motivation for comprehension and thus the construction of conceptual knowledge. In fact, a number of investigators with differing theoretical orientations have found that peer discussion and decision making facilitate meaningful learning, understanding, and cognitive growth (Inagaki, 1986; Perret-Clermont, 1980; Smith, Johnson, and Johnson, 1981).

Therefore, it is reasonable to assume that frequent dialogical interaction tends to lead to adaptive expertise. In addition to the three motivational conditions mentioned above, the following fourth condition might be appended:

4. *The procedures are used often in dialogical interaction.* One is likely to seek justifications and explanations much more often in dialogical interaction than in solitary activity.

## Applications of the Model

The above model of adaptive expertise can be applied to some domains of mathematical problem solving in an attempt to predict what type of experts students are likely to become from the four motivational conditions.

***What Do Abacus Learners Fail to Acquire?*** If, in the course of acquiring expertise (1) one is given the same types of problems repeatedly, (2) efficiency is valued much but understanding is not, (3) always getting the right answer is required, and (4) procedures are seldom used in the dialogical context (that is, none of the four conditions for adaptive expertise is satisfied), one will necessarily become no more than a routine expert. A typical case of such routine expertise is expertise in mental abacus operation.

A large number of Japanese children learn abacus operation in addition to paper-and-pencil calculation. They use an abacus that has a five-unit bead in the upper section and four one-unit beads in the lower section in each column. The numbers 0 through 9 are represented by "entering" (pushing toward the dividing bar) different combinations of beads. Addition and subtraction are done by pushing beads toward and away from the bar, with a few rules regarding carrying and borrowing. For example, if an addend needs more beads than available, add 1 to one column left and subtract the complementary number-to-10 of the addend from the target column (see Figure 1).

Figure 1. An Example of Addition with an Abacus: 9 + 8 = 17

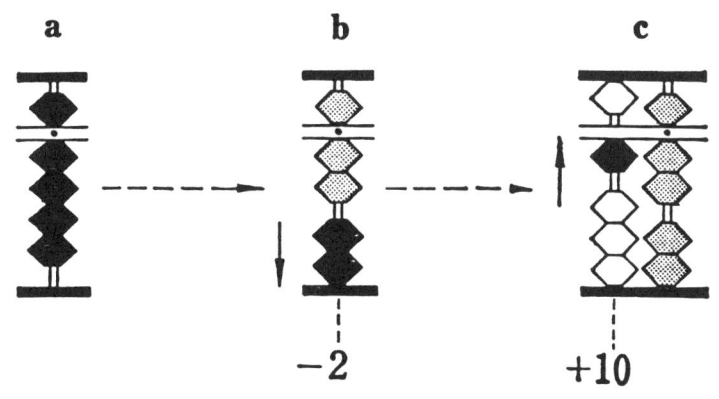

a. Enter 9.
b. You cannot add 8 in the ones column which has 9. So remove the complementary number-to-10 of 8 (that is 2) from the ones column.
c. Add 1 to the tens column.

Abacus operation, still used daily at small shops, is usually learned at a private school specialized for it, though it is sometimes acquired through informal observations and teaching. At the school students are given many problems for the four calculations without having the meaning of each step of calculation explained to them in detail. Since one can learn how to operate the instrument in just a few hours, training afterward is geared almost entirely to accelerating the speed of the operation.

Some abacus learners in fact become extraordinarily quick in calculation. For example, a fourth-grade girl my associate and I observed could solve 30 printed multidigit multiplication problems, 3 digits by 3 digits (for instance, 148 × 395) or 4 digits by 2 digits (3,519 × 42), in 58 seconds. This alone was surprising, but her net calculation time was even shorter—she needed the total amount of time for writing the answers down.

Several mechanisms are offered to explain this speed of calculation based on results from a large number of experiments (Hatano, forthcoming). First, a set of specific rules ("If addend 6 cannot enter, add 1 to one column left and subtract 4 from the target column") replaces the general rule that involves a variable ("the complementary number-to-10 of the addend" varies depending on the addend), and then a few such specific rules are merged into a single rule to get the final state directly ("If 7 is to be added to 6, add 1 to one column left and leave 3 at the target column"). Second, the application of these merged specific rules becomes more and more automatic.

Third, sensorimotor operation on physical representation of abacus beads comes to be interiorized as mental operation on a mental representation of an abacus. By this, the speed of the operation is no more limited by the speed of muscle movement. Fourth, a module-like system to represent mentally a number or series of digits in a form of the configuration of abacus beads, which is activated without any conscious effort or decision making, is established. Fifth, the mental imagery of abacus becomes simplified, eliminating properties unnecessary for calculation (such as the color of beads), so that the abacus can be manipulated even more quickly. Finally, monitoring of the operation is removed to use one's processing capacity to speed up the operation itself, since an expert's calculation is so fast that calculating twice is simpler than monitoring.

It should be noted that this process of acceleration of calculation speed results in a sacrifice of understanding and of the construction of conceptual knowledge. It is hard to unpack a merged specific rule to find the meaning of any given step (for example, leaving 3 at the target column when 7 is added to 6). A number is represented only in terms of a simplified image of beads that does not have rich meaning. No mental resources are used to reflect on why the procedure works, since this reflection would slow down calculation.

There have been a few studies suggesting that intermediate abacus learners do not know the meaning of the steps of abacus operation and that even experts lack conceptual knowledge. For example, interviews with abacus-learning third-graders about why certain steps were performed in the operation revealed that after a year of practice at an abacus school, they could explain the multidigit subtraction procedure no better than their agemates who just started the practice (Amaiwa and Hatano, 1983).

Amaiwa (1987) examined whether another group of third-graders who had practiced abacus operation for a year could repair their "buggy" paper-and-pencil calculation procedures by transferring the knowledge about the abacus procedure. She required the students alternately to solve the same problems with paper and pencil and with an abacus and found that many of them continuously made incorrect responses by the former procedure but correct responses by the latter. Amaiwa interpreted this to mean that since the students did not understand the meaning of steps of "base" abacus operation, they could not derive specific pieces of information to repair the "target" paper-and-pencil procedure.

In other unpublished studies with experts and junior experts, Amaiwa and I have found that they were not flexible in the use of their skills. When they were given multiplication and division problems, some of which could be solved by using simplifying strategies ($99 \times 38 \longrightarrow 38 \times 100 - 38$; $9{,}250 \div 25 \longrightarrow 9{,}250 \times 4 \div 100 \longrightarrow 925 \times 4 \div 10$), they did not recognize this possibility and solved all the problems mechanically in the same way, though their calculation was still much faster than that of ordinary college students. Another study revealed that the experts could not transfer their skills to nonconventional abacuses that were for a base 6 or 12 system. They performed no better with these abacuses than college students who had had negligible experience with the standard abacus. We must conclude that abacus operators apply the calculation procedures thousands of times without comprehending why the procedures work, probably because they have not constructed conceptual knowledge of the base 10 and other systems of numbers.

*Abacus Operation and Street Mathematics.* Abacus operation can be compared with other informal mathematical practices that have developed under different motivational conditions. It is interesting to do such a comparison because it helps clarify the significance of the four motivational conditions for determining the course of expertise. "Street mathematics" in Brazil will be used as an example (Carraher, Carraher, and Schliemann, 1985).

Apparently, abacus operation and street mathematics have much in common: (1) Both are used almost exclusively for commercial activities; (2) both can be acquired without systematic teaching; (3) both are outside of the "official knowledge" taught in school. However, they are radically different in "semantic transparency"—that is, in the clarity of the meaning of each calculation step. Steps of street mathematics, or "oral mathematics" (Carraher, Carraher, and Schliemann, 1987), in general, are clear in meaning, because the representations manipulated therein are information rich, and the ways of manipulation are analogous to actual activity dealing with goods, coins, and notes. For example, in order to find the price for twelve lemons of Cr$5.00 each, a nine-year-old child who was an expert street mathematician counted up by 10 (10, 20, 30, 40, 50, 60) while separating out two lemons at a time (Carraher, Carraher, and Schliemann, 1985). Quite to the contrary, representations of numbers on an abacus, though visibly concrete, are impoverished in meaning, and the way of manipulation is just mechanical.

Moreover, Brazilian children can flexibly use street mathematics or oral mathematics procedures. Oral computation procedures, often relying on decomposition and regrouping, generally reveal "solid understanding of the decimal system" (Carraher, Carraher, and Schliemann, 1987, p. 83)—that is, conceptual knowledge. Thus street mathematicians can be adaptive experts, while abacus operators are always routine experts.

These differences in knowledge come from differences in the cultural context of the practice and resultant motivational conditions for acquiring expertise. More specifically, what is different is the function of each mathematical practice in commercial activities. Street mathematics is basically a means by which a vendor and a customer reach an agreement as to the total price. It is an interpersonal enterprise that requires semantic transparency—otherwise the customer may be suspicious. Calculations cannot be performed very quickly, because they manipulate meaning-rich representations. However, the economy in which a young Brazilian vendor lives does not require high efficiency in calculation.

From the above analyses it can be assumed that (1) street mathematicians are posed novel types of problems fairly often because of changes in products, prices (as inflation increases), and customers' needs; (2) they are encouraged to seek comprehension as far as needed to explain to the customer the process of calculation; (3) accuracy of calculation is required, but not excessively, because its semantic transparency helps the vendor and customer recognize possible errors in calculation; and (4) calculation is done mostly in dialogical context. If these assumptions are correct, the motivational conditions for Brazilian vendors are radically different from those for abacus learners.

In contrast, Japanese abacus operation is basically a solitary activity in which operators handle large numbers quickly and accurately. Experienced abacus operators must be able to handle simplified representations, because the economy in which abacus operation developed required efficiency. A person or culture that values excessive efficiency must be content with simplified representations, giving up semantic transparency, understanding, and the construction of conceptual knowledge. Its operators are not interested in the semantic transparency of the calculation process either, because they believe that their skills ensure the correctness of the answer. Even when abacus operation is used in interpersonal situations of buying and selling, both the vendor and the customer are willing, in most cases, to accept the answers. Many Japanese customers and vendors seem to think that abacus operation is more dependable than calculation with a calculator.

***Some Instructional Implications.*** From the preceding discussion of the nature of abacus operation as a form of nonschool, or "informal," mathematics, two instructional implications can be derived. First, teachers must keep in mind that not every mathematics procedure that emerges in nonschool settings can serve as a basis for understanding how and why the corresponding school mathematics procedure works. Carraher and colleagues (1985) maintain mathematics learning in daily life produces effective and meaningful procedures that can complement potentially richer and more powerful mathematical tools acquired in school at the expense of meaning. However, daily life procedures are in fact semantically transparent—that is, the meaning of each step is understood by students only when the motivational conditions for their acquisition enhance the construction of conceptual knowledge.

I doubt that all (or nearly all) daily routines are meaningful—that is, clear—regarding why each step is needed. In principle, "our lives are filled with procedures we carry out simply to get things done" (Hatano and Inagaki, 1986, p. 266). Adults as well as children most likely perform some everyday problem-solving procedures only because they "work," without understanding the meaning of each step. If we repeat these steps hundreds of times, we can become quite skillful at them—that is, we can become routine experts. Pressing a key of a calculator to find the square root of a given number, like subtracting using an abacus, can be considered as one of such procedures.

Therefore, I doubt that it is always possible to find a semantically transparent informal procedure as the point of departure when we are to teach a formal one. We may need another strategy to make formal mathematics procedures meaningful. The second implication is relevant at this point. If we want to enable students to understand how and why school procedures work, we have to approximate the process of learning to the acquisition of street mathematics, not to expertise in abacus operation. In other words, we might encourage students to construct conceptual knowledge by providing the four motivational conditions that enhance it.

Although some traditional curriculum goals, such as efficiency in problem solving, accuracy, speed of calculation, and so on, must be sacrificed to some extent in order to pursue adaptive expertise, a majority of mathematics educators may be willing to do so if a model system of instruction for adaptive expertise is available. Such a model system is a Japanese science education method called Hypothesis-Experiment-Instruction, originally devised by Itakura (1962). A few people in Itakura's research group have applied the same instructional procedure to mathematics and limited areas of social studies. Hypothesis-Experiment-Instruction creates conditions for conceptual knowledge acquisition by maximally utilizing classroom discussion as well as by carefully sequencing problems.

The instructional procedure is as follows:

1. Students are presented with a question with three or four answer alternatives.

2. Students are asked to choose one answer by themselves.

3. Students' responses, counted by a show of hands, are tabulated on the blackboard.

4. Students are encouraged to explain and discuss their choices with one another.

5. Students are asked to choose an alternative once again (they may change their choices).

6. Students are allowed to test their predictions by observing an experiment (or reading a given passage).

Each answer alternative of a question represents a plausible idea, for example, a common misconception held by students as well as the correct one. Such a question will surely induce perplexity and discoordination.

It is also emphasized that students can clearly confirm or disconfirm their predictions by external feedback. Since questions arranged at the beginning part of a topic are likely to have right answers that contradict students' "modal" predictions based on their prior knowledge, they will experience surprise with the feedback.

If you visit a classroom in which Hypothesis-Experiment-Instruction is implemented successfully, you will be impressed by lively discussions in a large group of forty to forty-five students. You will recognize that the teacher is a facilitator who tries to stay as neutral as possible during students' discussion. This neutral attitude of the teacher is effective for encouraging students to seek comprehension and also for reducing their need to get external reinforcement, because pupils are invited to offer persuasive arguments to other pupils instead of seeking the right answer authorized by the teacher.

A few studies examining the effectiveness of this method (Hatano and Inagaki, 1987b; Inagaki and Hatano, 1968, 1977) have shown that the preceding six-step procedure tends to produce (1) higher student interest in testing their predictions or finding explanations, (2) a larger number of adequate explanations of the observed fact or stated rule, and (3) more prompt and more proper application of the learned procedure to a variety of situations. Many anecdotal reports strongly suggest that students taught in this method of instruction gradually come to think that understanding the how and why is more important than making the correct predictions. Therefore, although there is no direct evidence that students taught by Hypothesis-Experiment-Instruction tend to become adaptive experts in school science and mathematics, it seems a promising model system.

## Conclusion

A model of adaptive expertise suggests four conditions under which students, while using procedures for solving a large number of problems, are motivated to comprehend the procedures and thus acquire conceptual knowledge. These conditions are (1) encountering novel types of problems continuously, (2) being encouraged to seek comprehension over efficiency, (3) freedom from urgent need to get external reinforcement, and (4) dialogical interaction. When none of these conditions are met, as in the case of abacus operation, students are very unlikely to acquire the conceptual knowledge enabling them to understand the meaning of procedures though they are skilled in the procedures. On the contrary, when these conditions are satisfied more or less adequately, as in the case of Brazilian street mathematics, learners are likely to achieve understanding and flexibility of procedures.

Although we need more direct and controlled tests, these motivational conditions seem important for the development of mathematical understanding in instruction.

## References

Amaiwa, S. "Transfer of Subtraction Procedures from Abacus to Paper and Pencil" (in Japanese with English summary). *Japanese Journal of Educational Psychology*, 1987, *35*, 41-48.
Amaiwa, S., and Hatano, G. "Comprehension of Subtraction Procedures by Intermediate Abacus Learners" (in Japanese). Paper presented at the forty-seventh annual convention of the Japanese Psychological Association, Tokyo, September 1983.
Berlyne, D. E. "Motivational Problems Raised by Exploratory and Epistemic Behavior." In S. Koch (ed.), *Psychology: A Study of a Science*. Vol. 5. New York: McGraw-Hill, 1963.
Berlyne, D. E. "Curiosity and Education." In J. D. Krumboltz (ed.), *Learning and the Educational Process*. Chicago: Rand McNally, 1965a.
Berlyne, D. E. *Structure and Direction in Thinking*. New York: Wiley, 1965b.
Carey, S. *Conceptual Change in Childhood*. Cambridge, Mass.: MIT Press, 1985.
Carraher, T. N., Carraher, D. W., and Schliemann, A. D. "Mathematics in the Streets and in Schools." *British Journal of Developmental Psychology*, 1985, *3*, 21-29.
Carraher, T. N., Carraher, D. W., and Schliemann, A. D. "Written and Oral Mathematics." *Journal for Research in Mathematics Education*, 1987, *18*, 83-97.
Chi, M.T.H., Glaser, R., and Rees, E. "Expertise in Problem Solving." In R. J. Sternberg (ed.), *Advances in the Psychology of Human Intelligence*. Vol. 1. Hillsdale, N.J.: Erlbaum, 1982.
Gentner, D., and Stevens, A. L. (eds.). *Mental Models*. Hillsdale, N.J.: Erlbaum, 1983.
Glaser, R. "On the Nature of Expertise." In F. Klix and H. Hagendorf (eds.), *Human Memory and Cognitive Capabilities: Mechanisms and Performances*. Amsterdam: Elsevier Science Publishers B. V., 1986.
Greeno, J. G. "Forms of Understanding in Mathematical Problem Solving." Paper presented at the twenty-second International Congress of Psychology, Leipzig, East Germany, July 1980.
Hatano, G. "Becoming an Expert in Mental Abacus Operation: A Case of Routine Expertise" (in Japanese with English translation). In Japanese Cognitive Science Society (ed.), *Advances in Cognitive Science*. Vol. 1. Tokyo: Kodansha Scientific Publishers, in press.
Hatano, G., and Inagaki, K. "Two Courses of Expertise." In H. Stevenson, H. Azuma, and K. Hakuta (eds.), *Child Development and Education in Japan*. New York: W. H. Freeman, 1986.
Hatano, G., and Inagaki, K. "Everyday Biology and School Biology: How Do They Interact?" *Quarterly Newsletter of the Laboratory of Comparative Human Cognition*, 1987a, *9*, 120-128.
Hatano, G., and Inagaki, K. "A Theory of Motivation for Comprehension and Its Application to Mathematics Instruction." In T. A. Romberg and D. M. Stewart (eds.), *The Monitoring of School Mathematics: Background Papers*. Vol. 2: Implications from Psychology; Outcomes of Instruction. Program report 87-2. Madison: Wisconsin Center for Education Research, 1987b.
Hiebert, J., and Lefevre, P. "Conceptual and Procedural Knowledge in Mathe-

matics: An Introductory Analysis." In J. Hiebert (ed.), *Conceptual and Procedural Knowledge: The Case of Mathematics.* Hillsdale, N.J.: Erlbaum, 1986.

Inagaki, K. "Effects of External Reinforcement on Intrinsic Motivation" (in Japanese with English summary). *Japanese Psychological Review,* 1980, *23,* 121-132.

Inagaki, K. "Peer Interaction and Motivation for Understanding." Paper presented at Laboratory of Comparative Human Cognition seminar, "Cognitive Science in International Perspective." University of California, San Diego, April 1986.

Inagaki, K., and Hatano, G. "Motivational Influences on Epistemic Observation" (in Japanese with English summary). *Japanese Journal of Educational Psychology,* 1968, *16,* 191-202.

Inagaki, K., and Hatano, G. "Amplification of Cognitive Motivation and Its Effects on Epistemic Observation." *American Educational Research Journal,* 1977, *14,* 485-491.

Itakura, K. "Instruction and Learning of Concept Force in Static Based on Kasetsu-Jikken-Jugyo (Hypothesis-Experiment-Instruction): A New Method of Science Teaching" (in Japanese). *Bulletin of the National Institute for Educational Research,* 1962, *52,* 1-121.

Lepper, M. R. "Extrinsic Reward and Intrinsic Motivation: Implications for the Classroom." In J. M. Levine and M. C. Wang (eds.), *Teacher and Student Perception: Implications for Learning.* Hillsdale, N.J.: Erlbaum, 1983.

Lepper, M. R., and Greene, D. (eds.). *The Hidden Cost of Reward.* Hillsdale, N.J.: Erlbaum, 1978.

Markman, E. M. "Comprehension Monitoring." In W. P. Dickson (ed.), *Children's Oral Communication Skills.* Orlando, Fla.: Academic Press, 1981.

Miyake, N. "Constructive Interaction and the Iterative Process of Understanding" (in Japanese). *Cognitive Science,* 1986, *10,* 151-177.

Motoyoshi, M. *Essays on Education for Day Care Children: Emphasizing Daily Life Activities.* Tokyo: Froebel-kan, 1979.

Perret-Clermont, A. N. *Social Interaction and Cognitive Development in Children.* London: Academic Press, 1980.

Smith, K., Johnson, D. W., and Johnson, R. T. "Can Conflict Be Constructive? Controversy Versus Concurrence Seeking in Learning Groups." *Journal of Educational Psychology,* 1981, *73,* 651-663.


*Giyoo Hatano is professor of psychology and cognitive science at Dokkyo University, Saitama, Japan. He serves as an editorial board member of several developmental and cognitive journals.*

*Mathematics is a stumbling block in school for many children, yet the same children seem to acquire considerable mathematical knowledge without systematic teaching in everyday life. How can this discrepancy in performance be understood?*

# Mathematical Concepts in Everyday Life

*Terezinha N. Carraher, Analucia D. Schliemann, David W. Carraher*

The issue of the similarities and differences among concepts developed under distinct circumstances is an important one in developmental psychology, arising in various forms in different research contexts—such as in cross-cultural comparisons that deal with the same concepts learned in different cultures, in investigations of the transfer of knowledge from one content to another, or in studies of the transfer of knowledge from one social situation to another (such as from school to everyday life or vice versa). Despite considerable interest in the issue, developmental psychology still lacks an adequate theoretical framework for relating concepts to the circumstances in which learning takes place. The Piagetian stage theory is the framework most often used in cross-cultural comparisons (see, for example, Dasen, 1977) because it allows for the identification of similarities (same underlying logico-mathematical structures) despite differences in cultures. However, variations within subjects across domains of knowledge or across social situations challenge the "individual consistency" assumption basic to Piagetian stage theory—or basic to any structural description, for that matter.

Some within-individual variations were, of course, already acknowledged by Piagetians for different contents involving the same structure; the term *horizontal decalage* was coined to refer to intra-individual variation in performance, although the expression did not add much to our understanding of the issue. Later, Piaget and Garcia (1971) proposed a cognitive explanation for the horizontal decalage, according to which development involved a progressive differentiation of the logico-mathematical structures from their contents; some contents, being more complex, are differentiated from the underlying structures later than the simpler ones. However, this explanation leaves no room for cultural practices and social situations to play a role in cognitive tasks, and questions related to transfer across social situations remain unanswered.

There is considerable evidence of within-individual differences. Carraher, Carraher, and Schliemann (1985), for example, observed that children who worked as street vendors were quite capable of solving arithmetic problems in the streets but appeared inept at solving problems involving the same arithmetic operations in a school-like setting. In different social situations, the same children show radically different performance in solving problems that relate to the same domain and presumably call into play the same logico-mathematical structures. Lave, Murtaugh, and de la Rocha (1984) have also found large within-individual differences among adults solving problems across situations: highly instructed adults in California solved problems much better in the supermarket than on a mathematics test. How can one understand substantial within-subject variation across social situations for the same type of problems? In other words, how is it possible that people who know how to solve a problem in one situation do not know how to solve the same problem in another situation?

In this chapter we will explore the relationship between concepts and the circumstances of learning in an attempt to understand questions related to within-individual variation. Vergnaud's (1983) framework will be used for analyzing how concepts relate across situations. After presenting Vergnaud's basic ideas, we will use them to analyze some of our previous results on mathematical concepts in and out of school, discussing their similarities and differences. The first set of data refers to the solution of arithmetical problems. The second set concerns the solution of problems involving proportional reasoning.

According to Vergnaud, a concept necessarily entails a set of invariants, which constitute the properties defining the concept, a set of signifiers, which are a particular symbolic representation of the concept, and a set of situations, which give meaning to the concept. Due to the centrality of these three terms for the present analysis, we will consider each of them more closely.

In the case of mathematical concepts, invariants correspond to mathematical properties. For example, commutativity, associativity, and the existence of an identity operator are the defining properties (or invariants) for the operation of addition. People often behave as if they knew about these invariants in the course of solving addition problems. For example, if a child solves the problem "Mary had 3 marbles; she got 9 from her father; how many does she have now?" by counting three fingers up from nine (that is, solves 9 + 3 instead of 3 + 9), thereby inverting the order of the numbers in the story, one can infer that the order of the addends is being treated as irrelevant. In this case, the child's behavior indicates an implicit knowledge of commutativity as an invariant in addition.

A concept does not apply to one situation only but to several situations that give meaning to the concept. If two children recognize the same invariants in addition, for example, but do so for different situations, they are viewed, within Vergnaud's framework, as having different concepts because of the differences in the extension of their concepts. This is a new and important idea that Vergnaud introduces into conceptual analysis. Psychologists often view the defining properties of a concept as central aspects of concepts and extension as merely as epiphenomenon. Using addition once more as an example, the importance of situations in defining a concept can be clarified. Young children (about 6 years old) may understand the basic properties of addition and use them in solving problems. However, the set of situations to which addition is applied by six-year-olds tends to be limited. These young children fail to see that some problem situations are also solved by addition—for example, the problem "Mary has 3 marbles; she has 9 marbles less than Patricia; how many marbles does Patricia have?" Children who fail to see that addition is the numerical calculus required to solve this problem may know, as older children do, the addition invariants but have a different extension for the concept of addition—and consequently a different meaning.

A concept necessarily requires some form of representation for the subject's own use or for communication with others. A mathematical concept may be represented, for example, through graphs, equations, or natural language. Any representation is always only one of the possible representations of the same concept. Different representations of a concept tend to capture, in a clear fashion, different aspects of the concept. For example, the signifiers + and − refer to arithmetic operations—that is, a numerical calculus to be carried out in order to solve a problem. These signifiers do not represent the distinctions between situations in which the respective operations are useful. The word *situations* is used in two ways to mean (1) the problem-situations, included in Vergnaud's analysis, which must be analyzed in terms of the invariants that the subject brings to bear on the organization of his or her actions, and (2) the social situations, which often are involved in determining what type of signifiers will be used for interpersonal communication and representation. The sign -, for example, is used in situations in which we take away something, describe a debt, carry out a comparison, refer to temperatures below zero, and so forth. If all we know about a problem is that it involves -5, we cannot know what situation it refers to; the mathematical representation does not allow us to identify the particular problem-situation referred to. When a characterization of differences in situations is necessary, other symbolic representations have to be introduced—like language.

Let us now use Vergnaud's framework to address the issues of within-subject differences and the transfer of knowledge learned in one situation to another. We will review data from our work on mathematics learned in and out of school in order to examine whether the same invariants underlie the concepts learned in either setting, whether the use of different types of symbolic representation can account for within-individual differences across situations and whether street and school concepts differ in their generalizability across contents. The first set of data concerns arithmetic operations, and the second set deals with proportional reasoning.

**Arithmetic Operations**

We will discuss in this section data from two studies of children's abilities in solving arithmetic operations. The children in the first study (Carraher, Carraher, and Schliemann, 1985) were engaged in the informal sector of the economy, selling fruits, vegetables, or popcorn. They had experience with arithmetic problem solving in and out of school. In their work as street vendors, they calculate the total costs of purchases (for example, the cost of twelve lemons and two avocados) and the change due to their customers. In school they solve computation exercises and word problems. These two social situations—street vending and schooling—play a role in determining what type of symbolic representation is used for communication. In Brazilian street markets, written procedures are rarely used for calculating change. The currency itself supports the process of calculation: the vendor hands over the bills one by one to the customer while adding on (for example, 500 - 345 may be solved as "three hundred forty-five, fifty, four hundred, five hundred"). In schools, by contrast, written calculation is required: correct numerical answers without the proper written calculation tend to be disregarded by teachers.

Children who are street vendors thus learn about arithmetic operations under two different circumstances. Do they construct different invariants for their work in and out of school? Should the difference in signifiers—written versus oral—affect their performance, or are the differences between oral and written modes irrelevant to how mathematical knowledge is used in problem solving?

In our first study (Carraher, Carraher, and Schliemann, 1985), we investigated the arithmetic problem-solving ability of five youngsters (aged nine to fifteen years, with levels of schooling ranging from first to eighth grade) in three conditions. In the streets, the youngsters were given problems in the course of a commercial transaction between the vendor and the experimenter-as-customer. The experimenter posed problems about actual or possible purchases. For example, if the experimenter purchased Cr$135 (135 cruzeiros) of goods and paid with a Cr$200 bill, the child would have to determine the result of 200 − 135. The problems of the street situation served as a basis for generating word problems and computation exercises, which were later presented to the same subjects in a school-like fashion.

Striking within-subject variation in accuracy appeared across conditions: in the street 98 percent of the responses were correct. This compares to 74 percent when children worked on word problems and 37 percent correct answers on the computation exercises. (The difference between the children's performance in the street and in computation exercises was statistically significant.) While many differences across situations might account for the differences in performance (for example, the experimenter-child relationship was different in the two situations), we noted qualitative differences in how the children represented the problems in the street and in the school-like situation. Without exception, the children solved the problems in the street mentally, while in the school-like situation they often used paper and pencil. We hypothesized that form of representation—oral versus written—had a strong impact on the differences in performance. The following protocol illustrates one of the typical differences:

> Street Condition
> *Customer:* I'll take two coconuts *(each coconut costs Cr$40 and the customer pays with a Cr$500 bill).* What do I get back?
> *Child (before reaching for the customer's change):* Eighty, ninety, one hundred, four hundred and twenty.
>
> Formal Condition
> Test item: *What is 420 + 80?* The child writes 420 plus 80 and obtains 130 as the result. (The child lowers the 0 and then apparently proceeds as follows: adds the 8 + 2, carries the 1, and then adds 8 + 5, obtaining 13. The result is 130. Note that the child is applying steps from the multiplication algorithm to an addition problem.)

In the above example, the same child approaches the "same" problem (420 + 80) in distinct ways, in the street by "adding on" and in the school-like situation by unsuccessfully applying an algorithm learned in school.

In a second study (Carraher, Carraher, and Schliemann, 1987) conducted with sixteen third-grade children (none of whom were street vendors), some differences across situations were minimized. The experimenter was always an experimenter, not a customer, and the children were tested in their school. Three interviewing conditions, counterbalanced to avoid order effects, were used for all children: a simulated store condition in which the experimenter pretended to buy small items from the children, a word-problem condition, and a computation exercise condition. The numbers in the arithmetic operations were the same across situations for different children, so that differences across conditions could not be attributed to differences in the values involved in the problems. Paper and pencil were always available, but children could solve the problems in any way they wanted.

Significant differences in performance were again observed across examining conditions. First, experimental conditions were strongly related to the solution strategy. Children solved problems orally for over 80 percent of the simulated store problems and for 50 percent of the word problems but for less than 15 percent of the computation exercises. Further, in each condition, oral calculations had higher success rates than written calculations. A repeated measures analysis of variance revealed significant differences in the percentage of correct responses as a function of testing condition: children were more successful in the verbal problems than in the computation exercises and most successful in the simulated store condition. At first glance this would seem to suggest that children performed better under more concrete conditions. However, when the oral and written procedures are separated within conditions, the differences in success across conditions disappear. Thus the differences across conditions seem to be mediated by the type of solutions spontaneously adopted—oral or written. In other words, the same children solving problems that required the same operations but using different representations showed very different performance.

The oral procedures used by the sixteen children were then analyzed more closely in order to understand why the symbols used in problem solving made such a difference. Two general heuristics, decomposition and repeated groupings, were identified through this analysis.

Decomposition, used mostly for adding and subtracting, consists of breaking down the numbers into parts (usually separating hundreds from tens and units) and operating on these parts sequentially. The following protocol exemplifies this heuristic.

> The child was solving a word-problem in which the subtraction 200 - 35 was required. She said out loud: "If it were 30, then the result would be 70. But it is 35. So, it's 65, 165." The child decomposed the problem 200 - 35 into steps that seem to be the following: (1) 200 is the same as

100 + 100; (2) 100 - 30 is 70; (3) 70 - 5 is 65; finally, (4) adding the 100, which had been "set aside," as some children say, 165 [Carraher, Carraher, and Schliemann, 1987].

Decomposition can be compared to the borrowing algorithm taught in Brazilian schools through a similar analysis into steps so that differences that result from adding or subtracting orally or in writting can be identified and the invariants implicit in the two types of solution can be analyzed. Children using the borrowing algorithm would write the number 200, write 35 underneath aligned from the right, and then go through the following steps: (1) 0 - 5, you can't—borrow from the tens; (2) there are no tens—borrow from the hundreds; (3) take one (from the hundreds) and add it here (to the tens); (4) now borrow one (ten) and add it here (to units); (5) now subtract the number of units, tens and hundreds. The school algorithm can be rewritten as (1) 200 is the same as 190 + 10; (2) 10 - 5 is 5; (3) 9 (from 190) - 3 is 6; (4) 1 - 0 is 1; (5) read solution as 165.

The invariants implicit in the written and oral strategies can be stated as follows: a number is treated as composed of parts that can be separated without altering the total value; addition and subtraction can then be carried out on these parts without affecting the final result. This corresponds to the property of associativity—that is, the invariant underlying decomposition and addition or subtraction through written algorithms appears to be the same. (See Resnick, 1986, for a similar analysis with an American child.)

Despite the use of the same invariant, differences can be pointed out that result from the use of oral or written signifiers. In the oral mode, the relative value of numbers is pronounced: we say two hundred and twenty-two. In the written mode, the relative value is represented through relative position: we write 2, 2, 2. This difference in the signifiers is maintained in the calculating procedures: oral procedures preserve the relative values; written procedures set them aside. This is clearly shown in the protocol below in which the same child solved the same problem in the oral and then in the written mode. P.S., a third-grader, is asked to solve the computation exercise 200 - 35.

> P.S.: That's easy, one hundred and sixty-five *(does not write it down).*
> E.: How did you do it so quickly?
> P.S.: Two hundred, minus thirty, one seventy. Minus five, one sixty-five.
> E.: Can you do it on paper?
> P.S.: OK, I've learned it. I used to know this. *(Writes down, 200 the minus sign, 35 properly aligned underneath, and underlines.)* Zero minus five, carry the one. *(Writes down 5 as the result for units.)* Carry the one *(writing down 7, apparently calculating 10 - 3).* Carry the one. Two minus one. One. *(Writes down 1; the obtained result was 175.)*

The protocol clearly illustrates the within-subject difference we have been discussing; the child solved the computation correctly in the oral mode, preserving relative value during the process of calculation. When attempting the same problem in writing, the relative value was set aside and the wrong answer was obtained. The within-individual difference is all the more striking when the ease with which the child solves the computation in the oral mode is compared with the loss of meaning in the algorithmic procedure. Many children appeared quite lacking in ability when only their written attempts were considered, although they appeared quite at ease with numbers when only their oral calculations were taken into account.

Oral and written procedures also differ in the direction of calculation; the written algorithm is performed working from units to tens to hundreds, while the oral procedure follows the direction hundreds to tens to units.

A different heuristic, termed *repeated groupings,* was used for multiplication and division. It involves repeated additions, in the case of multiplication, and subtractions, in the case of division. Repeated grouping, like the multiplication algorithm, relies on distributivity as an implicit invariant—as can be noted in this example of a child calculating 15 × 50 in the simulated-store condition: "Ten (cars) will be five hundred; five, two hundred and fifty; seven hundred and fifty" (Carraher, Carraher, and Schliemann, 1987).

The child used in this multiplication the same groups we use in the written multiplication algorithm, namely, 5 and 10. However, his oral multiplication was performed in the opposite order, using 10 and then 5 as factors. Further, the factor 10 preserved its relative value, 10 being pronounced as *dez* (ten) instead of *um* (one). Thus multiplication and division replicate the previous observations with addition and subtraction: the invariants underlying the operations are the same, but the oral signifiers maintain an explicit representation of relative value and involve calculating in the direction hundred-tens-units, while with written signifiers, relative value is set aside and calculation proceeds from units to tens to hundreds.

The analysis so far has treated children's oral strategies as involving implicit invariants, granting these strategies the status of conceptual knowledge. However, it is possible that children behave as if they used associativity, commutativity, and distributivity but, in fact, they just have memorized procedures for calculating. Hatano (1982) applied the distinction between procedural and conceptual knowledge to the analysis of arithmetic operations, claiming that it is possible for subjects to learn how to carry out operators with the abacus without developing the corresponding conceptual knowledge operations—displaying, thus, simply procedural knowledge. Procedural knowledge was, in this case, the knowledge that allowed subjects to carry out operations correctly and efficiently but was neither flexible nor showed transfer to other situations.

Is it possible that the children who know oral mathematics merely know routines for calculating? The flexibility of oral mathematics seems to be too great to fit the idea of simple routines; in fact, it is only by overlooking much variability of particular steps that general descriptions of oral heuristics are possible. This flexibility contrasts strongly with the rigidity of the school-taught procedures, which may indeed be followed as routines without the corresponding comprehension. Cunha (1983), Ginsburg and Allardice (1984), Hart (1986), and Miranda (1987) have independently found that many children can carry out school-taught routines for adding and subtracting without understanding their meaning. Many children believed that the "one" they borrow or carry from one column to the next is worth one unit (although it always represents relative values different from the unit).

We have so far examined the concepts of arithmetic operations. It has been argued (Resnick, 1986) that children can learn these concepts outside school because the concepts are based on the additive composition property of numbers; more complex concepts, such as ratio and proportions, could not be understood in the absence of school instruction. In the next section, two studies on the understanding of proportional relations developed outside school are analyzed. The first study (Carraher, 1986) analyzes foremen's abilities in dealing with proportions in the domain of blueprint drawings. The second study (Schliemann and Carraher, 1988) analyzes proportional reasoning among fishermen in the context of pricing and calculating net weight of seafood.

**Knowledge About Proportions Developed at Work**

The distinct nature of the invariants underlying additive and proportional relations can be understood by comparing the following two problems, the first belonging to the field of addition and the second comprising proportional relationships:

*Problem 1.* When John was 13, Peter was 26. John is now 23 years old. How old is Peter?
*Problem 2.* A wall drawn 6 cm long in a blueprint is 3 m long in reality. What is the real length of a wall, which is 10 cm long in the same blueprint?

In Problem 1, we know that the difference between the ages of two people is constant at any point in time; it is by maintaining this difference constant that we calculate Peter's age today. In Problem 2, we must assume that there is a proportional relation between the size of the wall in reality and its representation in the blueprint; it is by maintaining this proportional relation constant that we calculate the size of any wall in reality. The contrast between the two problems shows that the invariant underlying solution in the first problem (a constant difference) differs from the invariant in the second (a constant ratio).

Data from two professions will be considered in this section in order to assess whether illiterate or semischooled adults who solve proportions problems in everyday life do so by constructing the appropriate invariants or by using procedural knowledge acquired outside school. The studies explore the distinction between procedural and conceptual knowledge by testing for flexibility and transfer—which Hatano (1982) proposed as distinctive of conceptual knowledge. The test for the flexibility of the subjects' knowledge was carried out by inverting in the experimental task the problems that the subjects solve in everyday settings. For example, people who usually calculate costs of purchases know the price of their merchandise per kilo and have to determine how much a greater number of kilos will cost. They can solve these problems by repeated addition or by multiplication. In our experimental tasks, the subjects were told prices of larger amounts and asked to determine unit prices. Solving these problems would require division or subtraction—that is, the inverse of the usual procedures.

Transfer from everyday work was investigated in different ways. In the study about blueprints, which is described first, the transfer task requires the subject to solve problems with new scales, for which familiar procedures could not work. In the second study, with fishermen, we investigated the transfer from one content—the relationship between weight of unprocessed versus processed seafood.

*Foremen's Knowledge of Scales.* Working with blueprints, foremen learn about scales, which are a mathematical way of expressing the relationship between the dimensions as drawn and the dimensions in reality. For example, a scale that is labeled 1 by 50 (written as 1:50) is used on blueprints in which the dimension of a wall in the blueprint must be multipled by 50 if one wants to calculate the real-life dimension of that same wall—thus, a wall drawn as 6 cm long will be 6 × 50, that is, 300 cm, or 3 m long. Foremen in Brazil learn about scales on the job; they receive no training in school. In Recife the most common scales are 1:100, 1:50, and 1:20. Foremen use their knowledge of scales in setting up guidelines to demarcate internal and external walls of buildings, making sure that length, width, and angles match specifications on the blueprint. Although the life-size dimensions are often written on the blueprints next to the drawing of walls, it is not uncommon for foremen to have to calculate the width of a window or a hallway from the blueprint because that measurement was left out.

The foremen interviewed in this study ($n$ = 17) had between zero and twelve years of schooling; only three who had seven or more years of schooling might have studied proportions in school. The subjects were shown blueprints drawn to four different, unspecified scales and were asked to determine the life-size measures of some walls in the blueprints, starting with three pieces of information: the life-size value and measure on the blueprint for a certain wall (one data pair) and the measure on the blueprint for another wall. This task requires the foremen to invert their usual procedure in order to identify the scale used in the drawing. Of the four scales included in this study, two are used in the foremen's practice and two are not used at all—termed here *unknown scales*.

Two problem-solving strategies accounted for approximately 94 percent of the responses given by foremen. The first strategy was closely connected to foremen's practice. It consisted of a sequential test of hypotheses about which of the scales known from their work experience fit the data at hand. The protocol below, in which an unknown scale was presented, illustrates this method.

> *L.S. (working with the 1:33.3 scale and the data 9 cm/3 m = 15 cm/x):* Nine centimeters, 3 meters. This scale is . . . 1 by 50, no, that would be 4½ meters. *(Pause)* If you drew it like this, that is because it is correct. *(Pause)* Can't do it.
> *E.:* Why not? You solved all the others.
> *L.S.:* Because it doesn't work for 1 by 50, it doesn't work for 1 by 1 (meaning 1 by 100), and it doesn't work for 1 by 20. There are three types of scale, 1 by 50, 1 by 20, and 1 by 1. The simplest scale is 1 by 1; you don't have to work on it, you look at the centimeters and you know the meters. Now, 1 by 50 and 1 by 20 you have to calculate. Now, this one here, it shows 9 centimeters by 3 meters. I've never worked with this one. I've only worked with the other three [Carraher, 1986, p. 585].

This method, used by approximately 34 percent of the foremen with unknown scales, does not require the inversion of procedures we expected to observe. Foremen make predictions about wall size by following the same methods they would use if they actually knew the scale. To test a hypothesis is to behave as if the scale was a particular scale and to verify whether the expected result is correct. Since only known scales belong to the subjects' pool of hypotheses, problems with unknown scales cannot be solved—that is, there is not transfer. Thus, according to the criteria we adopted, hypotheses testing is a strategy that reflects procedural knowledge of scale problems; there is no evidence of conceptual knowledge or proportionality when subjects work by testing hypotheses. Since there are only a few scales used in everyday life, a procedure may be learned for dealing with each scale. Besides this basic knowledge, foremen would still need in our study a procedure for testing which scale is under consideration. We have no evidence for the need in everyday life of this testing procedure, since scales are always identified on the blueprints, and therefore we do not know how and why it would be learned.

The second method observed in the study we called "discovering the relation." Instead of starting from a known relation, subjects identified a simplified ratio ($1/x$ or $x/1$) and applied it to other cases either by multiplication or by rated addition (adding step by step corresponding amounts to each variable in the problem). An instance of solution through discovering the relation follows:

> *J.M. (an illiterate foreman with twelve years of experience on the job, working with the unknown scale 1:40 and the data 5 cm/2 cm = 8 cm/x):* On paper it is 5 centimeters. The wall is to be 2 meters. Now, one thing I have to explain to you. This is not a scale that we usually work with.
> *E.:* That's right.
> *J.M.:* This one we'll have to divide. We will take 5 centimeters here and here 2 meters. *(Irrelevant comments.)* This one is hard. One meter is worth 2½ centimeters. *(This is the simplified ratio.)* Two meters, 5 centimeters *(marking off the centimeters on the measuring stick and counting the corresponding meters).* Three meters, 7½, 3 meters, but there are 5 millimeters more. *(The subject proceeds all the way to the correct solution)* [Carraher, 1986, p. 536].

The subject first identified the relationship to be kept constant ("One meter is worth 2½ centimeters") and then applied it through a mixture of additions and multiplications to the problem values, finding the solution. Although the ratio identified by the subject is not the same as the formal description of the scale (which is 1:40), both descriptions work in terms of ratios. This method was used by 60 percent of the foremen when the problems involved unknown scales. There was no association between level of schooling and foremen's use of this method in the problems with unknown scales.

Unlike hypothesis testing, discovering the relation is a strategy that rests on the inversion of everyday procedures to obtain the simplified ratio and can be applied to new scales. It is both flexible and transferable, fitting the criteria we set up to identify conceptual knowledge.

It can be concluded that both conceptual and procedural knowledge may result from practice with solving proportions problems in everyday life. However, we have no explanation as to why some foremen seemed to develop procedural and others conceptual knowledge, since levels of schooling were not related to type of procedure used in solving problems.

*Fishermen's Mathematics.* An ongoing study on fishermen's use of proportional reasoning will be reported here briefly. Fishermen's activities in catching, storing, and selling fish, shrimp, or other types of seafood involve them in weighing, pricing, and estimating losses when the fish and seafood are processed (shelled or salted) and stored for later sale. In the community we observed, fishermen usually sell their catches to middlemen before storing, but in order to evaluate the prices they get for their catches, they keep track of market prices. They may have to treat the catch before selling—oysters and crabs are usually shelled before being sold, but shrimp may or may not be shelled; whitebait may be salted and dried before sold, or it may be sold fresh to middlemen. All this economic exchange requires fishermen to know the approximate rates of volume of unprocessed to processed fish and seafood. However, they do not calculate these volumes and just make rough estimates most of the time (for example, $x$ plates of unshelled crab are needed for a plate of crab filet if the crab is medium sized; $x$ kilos of fresh whitebait correspond to one kilo of salted and dried whitebait). They must also know how to calculate prices as a function of weight. Thus, they use proportional reasoning to calculate in one domain (price as a function of weight) but only to understand the relationship between the variables in the other domain (ratio of unprocessed to processed seafood). The everyday knowledge developed by fishermen provides us with a natural experiment. They must understand two different types of problem situations—ratios of weight to price and of unprocessed to processed seafood—but only calculate in one domain. Would this experience promote the development of an understanding of proportional relations, or do fishermen learn in their activities only routines to deal with familiar prices? Can they transfer their strategies for calculating prices to the domain of calculating weight of unprocessed or processed seafood?

We asked nineteen fishermen (seventeen men and two women with levels of instruction ranging from no schooling to incomplete secondary school) to solve three experimental tasks related to the understanding of proportions. Subjects were asked to (1) calculate unit prices when prices for larger numbers of units were given and were different from present market prices (that is, they had to invert their usual procedure, which goes from unit prices to prices of large amounts); (2) solve problems involving unknown rates of unprocessed to processed seafood, which requires the inversion of the usual procedure and transfer to a domain in which calculation is not used (that is, subjects were given the ratios for numbers of units larger than one and asked to calculate how much was needed for one unit of processed seafood); and (3) solve problems in which subjects were told the ratios of unprocessed to processed seafood for a larger number of units and had to fulfill a request by a customer that did not involve unit yield (for example, if you were to catch this type of shrimp that they have in the South that yields 3 kilos of shelled shrimp for every 18 kilos that you catch, how many kilos would you have to catch for a customer that only wants 2 kilos of shelled shrimp?).

Three problems of type 1, two of type 2, and three of type 3 were presented to subjects. Testing was done on different occasions when subjects could not continue testing after having completed one task. The data reported below include a total of 115 responses; missing data are due to difficulties in relocating subjects for completion of the tasks.

Overall performance was rather good: 78 percent of correct responses were observed for the prices questions (type 1 problems) in which subjects had to invert calculation routines they are used to; 77 percent correct for questions on unprocessed to processed ratios in which they had to transfer and invert procedures used in another domain but not normally used in this domain (type 2 problems); and 57 percent correct for questions requiring transfer of a relation to nonunitary quantities (type 3 problems). There was no relationship between years of schooling and ability to use proportional reasoning in any of the tasks—a result in keeping with the findings of the study with foremen.

These preliminary data on the use of proportional reasoning among fishermen suggest that they develop an understanding of proportional relations in their everyday practice, not just simple procedural knowledge to solve the problems they are faced with. They were able to both invert the computational strategies they use at work and to transfer them to domains in which they are usually not applied.

As in the study with foremen, the present study leads us to believe that learning mathematics outside school is not restricted to the field of additive relations; more complex concepts can also be developed. Further, concepts learned outside school are not restricted to the domain in which they are learned but can transfer to other domains.

It does not seem to be the case that the social situations in which concepts are learned—inside or outside school—determine concepts' nature or generalizability, although social situations have a strong impact on how concepts are represented.

**Conclusions**

Relating concepts to the circumstances in which they were learned requires looking at knowledge from different perspectives. First, the nature of the acquired knowledge must itself be understood. However, all we observe is behavior. How can we discover whether distinct types of knowledge underlie different types of behavior, all of which lead to success? The main criterion used here was flexibility. Knowledge that is not flexible was treated as procedural knowledge—and thus not justifying inferences regarding the existence of invariants implicit in the organization of the subjects' actions. Knowledge that is flexible was treated as conceptual knowledge. The nature of the knowledge used in problem solving has clear implications for within-subject variation, since procedural knowledge does not seem to transfer across domains.

Second, if subjects display conceptual knowledge through their problem-solving behavior, one would like to know what specific invariants are implicit in their behavior. There are often different routes to solving a problem. Are the same invariants implicit in the different routes, or are different routes based on different invariants? Detailed analysis of problem-solving strategies is needed for the identification of underlying invariants. The previous analyses of addition and subtraction, multiplication and division, and proportional reasoning support the idea that the same invariants can be constructed in distinct situations although great differences in problem-solving strategies may exist.

Third, social situations are a strong determinant of which symbolic representations are used in problem solving, owing to implicit social rules (or ideology); school mathematics is mostly written, and mathematics in the markets is mostly oral. Most people would be ready to acknowledge that success in many motor tasks, such as nailing and sawing, is partially determined by the tools we use, but psychologists often fail to consider the impact that different types of symbolic representation may have on thinking. These different symbolic systems influence the routes to problem solving, resulting in marked within-individual variation, despite the fact that the same invariants are needed for understanding oral and written calculation.

Finally, we would like to ask what implications for educational research can be drawn from studies of mathematical concepts learned outside school. Knowing that children and adults from poor backgrounds learn much about mathematics in everyday life without the benefit of systematic teaching is certainly a starting point for research in mathematical education. Perhaps the contribution of concrete situations—not concrete materials—to new pedagogical practices is worth investigating. Another aspect of mathematical education that seems worth investigating is what different types of representation may offer to conceptual learning if brought from everyday life into the classroom. Saxe (1982), for example, studied adults in Papua New Guinea who became involved in commerce and had to deal with the Australian monetary system. These adults soon began imposing on the indigenous numeration system, which was a nonbase system, the base 20 which reflected the organization of the Australian monetary system. This spontaneous reorganization of the indigenous numeration system under the influence of a monetary system suggests the possibility of attaining present educational goals through the introduction of out-of-school experiences into the classroom. Along these lines, Carraher and Schliemann (in press) discuss what role money as a representation of value may play in helping children understand the decimal system.

The present results show that neither abstract thought nor conceptual knowledge of mathematics is a privilege of those with many years of

Western schooling. However, mathematics brings pupils into contact with sophisticated symbolic systems not readily available outside the classroom—systems that certainly have an impact on the development of mathematical knowledge. If we are willing to set aside the models of intelligence presently used in education, which treat the processes of problem solving as properties of the individuals (see, for example, Cole, Gay, Glick, and Sharp, 1971), much exciting research can be carried out investigating the impact of mathematical symbolic systems on the development of knowledge. Mathematical concepts learned in school could then be studied as concepts learned as a result of specific cultural practices in much the same way that everyday mathematics is now being investigated.

**References**

Carraher, T. N. "From Drawings to Buildings: Working with Mathematical Scales." *International Journal of Behavioral Development*, 1986, *9*, 527-544.
Carraher, T. N., Carraher, D. W., and Schliemann, A. D. "Mathematics in the Streets and in Schools." *British Journal of Development Psychology*, 1985, *3*, 21-29.
Carraher, T. N., Carraher, D. W., and Schliemann, A. D. "Written and Oral Mathematics." *Journal for Research in Mathematics Education*, 1987, *18* (2), 83-97.
Carraher, T. N., and Schliemann, A. D. "Using Money to Teach About the Decimal System." *Arithmetic Teacher*, in press.
Cole, M., Gay, J., Glick, J., and Sharp, D. *The Cultural Context of Learning and Thinking*. New York: Basic Books, 1971.
Cunha, T.M.V. "O desenvolvimento dos conceitos de esquerda e de direita e da compreensão do sistema de numeracão decimal" [The development of the concepts of left and right and of the understanding of the decimal numeration system]. Master's thesis, Universidade Federal de Pernambuco, Recife, Brazil, 1983.
Dasen, P. R. *Piagetian Psychology: Cross-Cultural Contributions*. New York: Gardner, 1977.
Ginsburg, H. P., and Allardice, B. S. "Children's Difficulties with School Mathematics." In B. Rogoff and J. Lave (eds.), *Everyday Cognition: Its Development and Social Context*. Cambridge, Mass.: Harvard University Press, 1984.
Hart, K. "The Step to Formalization." In *Proceedings of the Tenth International Conference on Psychology of Mathematics Education*. London: University of London Institute of Education, 1986.
Hatano, G. "Cognitive Consequences of Practice in Culture-Specific Procedural Skills." *Quarterly Newsletter of the Laboratory of Comparative Human Cognition*, 1982, *4* (1), 15-18.
Lave, J., Murtaugh, M., and de la Rocha, O. "The Dialectic of Arithmetic in Grocery Shopping." In B. Rogoff and J. Lave (eds.), *Everyday Cognition: Its Development in Social Context*. Cambridge, Mass.: Harvard University Press, 1984.
Miranda, E. M. "O que as criancas precisam saber para aprender a fazer continhas de pedir emprestado?" [What do children need to know in order to learn the borrowing algorithm?] Master's thesis, Universidade Federal de Pernambuco, Recife, Brazil, 1987.

Piaget, J., and Garcia, R. *Les explications causales* [Causal explanations]. Paris: Presses Universitaires de France, 1971.

Resnick, L. B. "The Development of Mathematical Intuition." In M. Perlmutter (ed.), *Perspectives on Intellectual Development.* Vol. 19. Hillsdale, N.J.: Erlbaum, 1986.

Saxe, G. B. "Developing Forms of Arithmetic Operations Among the Oksapmin of Papua New Guinea." *Developmental Psychology,* 1982, *18* (4), 583–594.

Schliemann, A. D., and Carraher, T. N. "Everyday Experience as a Source of Mathematical Learning: Knowledge Complexity and Transfer." Paper presented at the 1988 annual meeting of the American Educational Research Association, New Orleans, La., 1988.

Vergnaud, G. "Multiplicative Structures." In R. Lesh and M. Landau (eds.), *Acquisition of Mathematics: Concept and Process.* Orlando, Fla.: Academic Press, 1983.

*Terezinha N. Carraher, Analucia D. Schliemann, and David W. Carraher are associate professors at the Universidade Federal de Pernambuco, Recife, Brazil. Their work includes a decade of studies of everyday mathematics published in* Na Vida, Dez; na Escola, Zero: Os Contextos Culturais de Aprendizagem da Matemática [Street math and school math: The cultural contexts of learning mathematics] *(1988).*

*The development of mathematical thinking involves more than cognition alone: affect, motivation, and personality are crucial.*

# Hot Mathematics

*Herbert P. Ginsburg, Kirsten A. Asmussen*

Cognitive explanations of mathematical thinking (and of other intellectual activities) are valuable but not sufficient. Narrow in focus, they overlook much that is central to children's and adults' mathematics learning. As other chapters in this volume show, cognitive explanations often fail to consider the ways in which mathematical thinking operates within the social context. Here we argue that they also ignore those aspects of mathematical experience involving feelings, motivations, and personal meanings—in short, what could be called "hot mathematics."

**The Problem and the Paradox**

The phenomenon to be explained is the widespread tendency for individuals, particularly in the United States, to experience serious difficulties in learning mathematics. They not only display low levels of achievement but also suffer from emotional distress surrounding their mathematics learning. The paradox is that these difficulties occur in otherwise intelligent individuals who possess important and surprising intellectual resources that ought to make mathematics learning relatively easy.

---

The authors wish to express appreciation to the Spencer Foundation for generous support of their work in this area. In addition they thank Alexandra Subrenat, then a graduate student at Teachers College, for her assistance in both interviewing and planning the study.

*Widespread Mathematics Learning Difficulties.* Evidence for mathematics learning difficulties in the U.S. population is abundant. Cross-national research has shown that from the elementary school years, U.S. children perform at a lower level on standard mathematics achievement tests than do children in other countries (Stevenson and others, 1985).

Not only do many individuals achieve poorly in mathematics, they also dislike and avoid it. By the third grade or so, children often say they "hate" mathematics; they seem to experience great discomfort when they must produce number facts quickly and correctly; and some children feel that mathematics is the dullest of school subjects, about as boring and senseless as spelling. The situation seems to get even worse after childhood. In high school and college, many adolescents take as few mathematics courses as they can get away with, seldom studying topics beyond algebra and, in many cases, arithmetic (McKnight and others, 1987). Some individuals even suffer from "math anxiety," an extreme fear and loathing of mathematics. One such person told us that when compelled to engage in mathematical work, she felt physically nauseous, on the verge of throwing up.

*The Paradox.* From a cognitive point of view alone, it is hard to understand why mathematics learning problems—low achievement and anxiety—should be so prevalent. Indeed, cognitive developmental theories suggest at least two reasons for believing that people ought not to have an especially difficult time in learning mathematics. The first is that the vast majority of children and adults possess sound basic intellectual processes—skills in reasoning, abstraction, memory, and the like. Thus, elementary school children doing poorly in arithmetic nevertheless possess the Piagetian thought structures, such as concrete operations, that ought to be sufficient for understanding the subject matter (Allardice and Ginsburg, 1983). Indeed, as Piaget ([1935] 1970) maintained, it is hard to understand why children have difficulty learning something that is in a sense merely an extension and formalization of what they already know.

We recognize of course that some individuals lack the basic intellectual equipment for learning mathematics. This must be true of many retarded persons. There may even be a few genuine cases of learning disability in mathematics (see for example McCloskey and Caramazza, 1985). But despite these exceptions, it is abundantly clear that for most individuals basic cognitive deficiency is not responsible for learning difficulties in mathematics, at least at the level of the primary and secondary school curriculum. The child does not fail in mathematics because he or she lacks concrete operations or has a faulty memory or a low IQ. Donaldson (1978) states this as a basic paradox: why should the young child, so abundantly blessed with intellectual resources and so deeply committed to learning and exploration of the world, act so stupidly after a few years of school? "The problem then is to understand how something that begins so well can often end so badly" (p. 6).

A second reason for expecting people to learn mathematics with relative ease is that virtually everyone begins school with at least adequate, if not sophisticated, knowledge of informal mathematis. Children from preliterate societies in Africa (Saxe and Posner, 1983), street children in Brazil (Carraher, Carraher, and Schliemann, 1985), and lower-class children in the United States (Ginsburg and Russell, 1981) all demonstrate competence in basic concepts and procedures of arithmetic. Further, given this basis of informal mathematics, children should not find it hard to learn what is taught in school. For example, even in preliterate cultures children spontaneously construct mental addition strategies embodying decomposition principles analogous to the base 10 system (Ginsburg, Posner, and Russell, 1981). Therefore, why should children capable of such sophisticated forms of mental addition experience difficulty learning the standard carrying algorithm? Yet they do.

The problem is not a lack of informal mathematics that can be a basis for understanding school mathematics but that children fail to relate the two. One of the most striking aspects of learning problems is a kind of "cognitive schizophrenia." We use this term to refer to the split state of mind in which many children fail to connect their informal knowledge—their mathematical common sense—with what they learn in school. For them, school mathematics is a separate domain of arbitrary "stuff" to be learned in meaningless ways. Thus, a child tries to figure out ways of manipulating collections of numbers in order to get some result, where both the numbers and result are meaningless (as in the case of the child who adds $100 + 1 = 200$) and does not relate to what is already known (namely that 100 things and 1 thing definitely do not add up to 200 things).

The paradox of learning difficulties in intelligent people is perhaps most dramatic in the person suffering from math anxiety. Most often, the math-anxious individual is competent and successful in a variety of academic areas, except for those involving mathematics (Brush, 1978), and is therefore restricted in the choice of academic pursuits and professional careers (Ernest, 1976).

We argue then that learning difficulties in mathematics do not often result from a lack of cognitive ability, either in the sense of defective general intellectual skills, such as concrete operations, or of a deficiency in informal mathematical knowledge. Learning difficulties certainly involve cognitive confusions and inadequacies, and even "cognitive schizophrenia." But the main cause of all these problems is not basic cognitive deficiency.

Another way of saying this is that mathematics learning difficulty is not an issue of competence in Piaget's sense, but one of performance.

Almost all of us possess the underlying structures of knowledge—that is, our shared competence—that should enable us to learn simple mathematics with relative ease. At the same time, many of us do not build on that competence to achieve successful performance. The basic question then is: what kind of factors interfere with our virtually universal intellectual abilities in such a way as to produce mathematics learning difficulties, both intellectual and emotional? What are the causes of the massive ignorance, fear, and loathing of a key area of human knowledge?

**Instructional Causes of Poor Achievement**

One obvious and serious explanation of learning problems refers to environmental impediments, specifically, an inadequate educational system. Mathematics teaching is often unclear: textbooks may present materials in confusing ways, teachers may not convey the idea that mathematics ought to make sense, and teachers may cover a variety of topics in a superficial manner rather than present any single topic in adequate depth (Stigler and Perry, 1987). Furthermore, many teachers themselves suffer from math anxiety and inadvertently transmit it to their students (Brush, 1981; Stodolsky, 1985). Given such inadequacies of mathematics education, it is no surprise that people have trouble learning math.

Although obviously influential, the quality of instruction cannot fully explain individual differences in educational achievement and in feelings and attitudes toward the subject matter. In the same classroom, some children learn mathematics reasonably well and others, despite adequate intellectual ability, learn it poorly; some like it and some hate it. Some individuals learn well even under poor instructional conditions, while others, despite adequate intellectual ability, fail to learn from good instruction. Also, a focus on instruction alone may not explain why some individuals who achieve well in the subject entertain such negative feelings toward learning mathematics.

Although the nature of instruction can make an important difference in mathematics learning, we must also consider the psychology of the individual receiving the instruction. We have seen that the typical individual most likely suffers from no basic cognitive defects that can account for the learning problems. We must therefore look for noncognitive explanations—which raises the issue of hot mathematics.

**Noncognitive Explanations**

Several writers have proposed going beyond the purely cognitive to consider issues of belief, motivation, style, affect, and identity. We begin with a brief discussion of the available literature concerning each of these factors or processes. We argue that although consideration of these factors broadens our understanding, we require a deeper and more complex view of how the various processes develop and operate in the context of personality so as to produce learning problems. We need a developmental "depth psychology." Only by developing such a theoretical framework, difficult and ambitious as the task may be, can we understand the complexity of mathematical performance (and intellectual performance, generally) in the real world. And perhaps such a framework will help us develop educational approaches designed to avoid squandering children's enormous intellectual potential. First, we consider how beliefs affect mathematical knowledge, and then we consider the roles of motivation, style, affect, and identity.

*Beliefs.* In the early school years children develop basic beliefs concerning the nature of mathematics, and these affect academic performance. For example, according to Baroody, Ginsburg, and Waxman (1983), some children come to believe that solving arithmetic problems must involve tedious computations, even if these could be entirely eliminated by appealing to reason or principle. These children consider that reasoning about arithmetic problems is undesirable; indeed it is "cheating." Similarly, some children—and teachers!—define knowing the number facts as necessarily involving quick, accurate response without any thought, which is somehow considered undesirable (Ginsburg, in press). The general belief, fostered by the educational system, is that mathematics is getting right answers in a thoughtless way, either through rote computation or memory.

It is not hard to see how this conception of mathematics can influence children's approach to the subject. The emphasis on accuracy and quick responses seems to produce anxiety in some children. And it may discourage others from using their informal knowledge (and reason, generally) to solve mathematics problems. This in turn may result in wrong answers, which may again produce feelings of anxiety, leading to an unending spiral of failure.

*Motivation.* Dweck's theory (Dweck and Elliot, 1983) is useful in considering some aspects of children's motivation for learning mathematics. They make a distinction between two major types of goal choices in learning situations. The child who selects a performance goal tends to focus on the external aspects of the learning situation and either tries to avoid failure or show off skills (if they are perceived to exist in the given situation). This theory predicts that performance-oriented children perceiving themselves as having poor or uncertain ability may avoid mathematics tasks or may give up quickly when having difficulty grasping the subject.

However, children who adopt a learning goal concentrate their attention on acquiring skills rather than concerning themselves with looking good or not looking bad. Often, these children become so involved in learning that they lose sight of whether or not they are succeeding. Dweck and Elliot predict that the learning-oriented child will persist in mathematics tasks, even when ideas are difficult to grasp or when mistakes are made.

Dweck and Elliot have also found that goal choices interact with the child's level of confidence. As long as confidence is high (in a given situation), even the child with a performance goal may demonstrate mastery-oriented behavior. However, the child who adopts the learning goal appears less vulnerable to mathematics difficulties, for regardless of whether confidence is high or low, this child's lack of concern with external judgments allows him or her to concentrate on learning the task at hand.

In addition, goal choices interact with the individual's notions of the roles of effort and ability. Those children who believe that intelligence is fixed—that it cannot be improved through effort—are likely to adopt a performance goal. The learning-goal child, however, believes that he or she is capable of increasing intelligence and, with this belief, concentrates on the act of learning itself.

Dweck (Dweck and Elliot, 1983; Dweck, Davidson, Nelson, and Enna, 1978) reports that a significant minority of children are characterized by a performance orientation and that most of these children are girls. This finding may be related to differences in feedback girls and boys receive from their teachers. Dweck, Davidson, Nelson, and Enna (1978) found that boys receive more criticism than girls and that the criticism pertains to boys' degree of effort: they do not try hard enough. When girls receive criticism, it more often pertains to intellectual ability: they are not smart enough. Thus, teaching may influence children's beliefs and goal choices, with important consequences for work in mathematics, a subject where persistence and effort are crucial for many children.

*Cognitive Styles and Strategies.* Another factor influencing mathematical performance is cognitive style. This concept refers to a "habit of thought" (Messick, 1984), a distinctive way of doing intellectual tasks. Theorists have proposed that many different cognitive styles—ranging from "risk-taking" to "field dependence" (Messick, 1984)—are useful for understanding intellectual performance in that they influence the manner in which individuals approach specific tasks and eventually learn (or fail to learn). Thus, a "rigid" but able person may learn only the standard algorithm and may fail to develop less orthodox, informal methods for solving computational problems. The results may be both high scores on achievement tests and a lack of ability to cope with novel problems. A dependent child may not do anything unless adults approve; this approach surely limits the chances of exploration. The "success" of a style depends partly on environmental circumstances; one may benefit from acting rigidly in certain situations but not in others. Many teachers and texts reward rigidity; some real-world job situations do not, such as, for example, Scribner's (1984) dairy plant. We also note that cognitive style is not defined directly in terms of ability but may depend on it; it is hard to exhibit flexibility of thought if one possesses few intellectual resources.

Cognitive style bears a close relation to study and organizational skills. Obviously, study pursued in a planful, organized, and careful manner is likely to result in improved performance (Brown, Bransford, Ferrara, and Campione, 1983). And study habits also interact with beliefs and goal choices. Given the task of learning the number facts, the rigid, performance-oriented individual may employ methodical techniques resulting, perhaps, in good test performance but in little understanding of what is memorized.

*Affect.* Emotional factors obviously affect intellectual performance in both positive and negative ways. With respect to the former, confidence—that is, good feelings about one's current performance and positive expectations concerning future performance—stands in a strong positive relation to mathematic achievement (Reyes, 1984), although direction of causality is not simple. No doubt, confidence may facilitate doing well, but doing well can also increase confidence. Thus, Bandura (1981) has suggested that feelings of self-efficacy are at least partially rooted in experiences of success and failure. To further complicate matters, according to Shiffler, Lynch-Sauer, and Nadelman (1977), students with high self-confidence spend more time than those with low confidence on mathematics tasks, and they interact more with teachers. They can thus learn more, which in turn can increase feelings of self-confidence.

On the negative side, anxiety can play an important role in impeding success. When some students perceive themselves to be in a potentially threatening learning situation, they experience anxiety, as revealed by certain physiological and behavioral signs (Reyes, 1984): an increase in heart rate, sweaty hands, muscle tension, and fidgety and nervous behavior. In some individuals, these reactions depress performance, one reason being that attention centers on the anxiety rather than on the task at hand.

*Identity.* Two lines of research point to the role of identity in learning. One involves the concept of self as a learner. In the early years of school, children develop clear notions of their abilities in particular academic areas. Entwistle and Hayduk (1978) have found that by the third grade many children have developed firm and negative views of themselves as learners. No doubt these learning identities both influence and are influenced by real learning experiences. Thus, doing well in arithmetic helps children see themselves as good learners, and this kind of identity contributes to successful performance. For example, one little boy told us repeatedly that he was very good in mathematics, and this concept of self appeared to facilitate his persistence, even when he was having difficulty performing various tasks. One's identity as a learner also seems to influence both choices of subjects to study and approaches to them.

Broader aspects of identity can also affect learning. This occurs in many ways, one of which involves sex-roles. For example, it has been reported that parents and teachers have differing expectations of boys and girls with regard to mathematics (Parsons, Adler, and Kaczala, 1982). Presumably, at least in some quarters, the cultural expectation is that success in mathematics is not a proper aspect of the girl's role. For adolescents this may translate into the belief that mathematics is primarily a male field (Stein, 1971; Sherman, 1980). Indeed, it was initially reported that girls consider mathematics less useful for future goals than do boys (Sherman, 1980). These beliefs may also be related to the lack of adequate female role models in mathematics-related areas (Ernest, 1976; Tobias and Weissbrod, 1980), although now the situation may be changing as more women enter mathematics and science-related fields (Benbow and Stanley, 1982). Nevertheless, cultural expectations seem to cause at least some girls to develop an identity in which mathematical success is seen as inappropriate: they then avoid mathematics and subsequently develop low self-confidence in it and related activities (Reyes, 1984). The issue here, then, is not simply one's concept of self as a learner but the role one's identity (gender, career, or other) plays in influencing mathematics learning.

*The Need for a Developmental and Dynamic Psychology.* Suppose that, as we have argued, mathematics learning difficulties cannot be explained in terms of a unitary notion of "math anxiety." Suppose further that as the evidence shows, each of the separate factors or processes described above—beliefs, motivation, and the rest—has some effect on mathematics achievement. All of this points us in interesting directions, broadening the scope of inquiry by introducing considerations of performance, as opposed to intellectual competence, which, as we have seen cannot explain most mathematics difficulties.

But consideration of beliefs, motivation, and the rest does not go far enough; many questions remain unanswered. First, there is very little information concerning the development of learning problems and of the factors contributing to them. When do learning problems manifest themselves, and what forms do they take over the course of development? Little research has been done on this matter. How do motivational constellations, such as a performance orientation, evolve over time? The Dweck theory is essentially a-developmental, providing no insight into the issue.

Second, we have little insight into the ways in which the various factors described above interact to produce learning difficulties. Although

Dweck and colleagues have made some beginning efforts in this area, attempting to show, for example, how beliefs about intelligence interact with performance goals to affect persistence, we know little about how cognitive style, for example, interacts with affect or identity to influence mathematics achievement. Perhaps another way of saying this is that we have little knowledge of the dynamics of the situation—how processes such as beliefs or motives function within the larger context of personality so as to affect learning. In brief, we lack a holistic approach that treats learning difficulties in the contexts of development and of personality.

Part of the reason for our ignorance of these matters is that psychological researchers' conventional methodology is to use groups of subjects, employ experimental design, and attempt to isolate the effects of variables. This method effectively prevents the consideration of complex interactions of processes in living, developing personalities. For these reasons, we employ the method of individual case study, a method particularly valuable when the aim is to explore an issue as complex as the development of learning problems. As we shall see, this method allows us to obtain some insight into the complex development of the affective and cognitive within the structure of personality.

**Method of Study**

Given the goal of exploring such issues, we chose to work in an informal and intense fashion with individual adults, since they might provide more insight than children into their learning histories and the causes of their problems. We conducted a series of eight sessions, lasting about one hour each, with each of six graduate student volunteers who identified themselves as suffering from math anxiety. Two of our participants were male and four female, all adults between the ages of 21 and 50. Each subject was seen by the same interviewer in all of the individual sessions. Three interviewers worked with the six subjects.

The first four sessions, employing as the main method a loosely structured interview technique, explored subjects' feelings toward mathematics and experiences with mathematics at home and in school and their recollections of parents' and teachers' attitudes toward mathematics achievement. Although the interviews were based on a protocol describing key questions to be asked and basic topics to be covered, the interviewer was allowed to introduce further questions as needed. In addition to the interviews, we administered a projective test (Mueller and Ginsburg, forthcoming) designed to examine conflicts and concerns centering around school as well as related emotional issues. We also administered the Math Anxiety Rating Scale (Richardson and Suinn, 1972) and afterward discussed with each individual his or her responses to the test.

Next followed a series of sessions in which we conducted clinical interviews concerning subjects' ongoing work with mathematics problems. The interviews were intended to provide information on cognitive processes employed in mathematical problem solving, on the influence of emotions and beliefs on mathematical performance, and on the role of cognitive style.

At the end, four group interviews were conducted. It was our hope that the supportive group interaction would help the individuals identify and articulate their concerns, feelings, and difficulties and that the sharing of such information would be useful to the individuals involved. Although it was not our purpose to provide deep therapy for our volunteers, all of them remarked that the interviews and group sessions had a beneficial effect, and some even reported a diminution of their fear of mathematics.

A second exploratory study took a similar form, but involved undergraduate volunteers who reported learning problems in a variety of areas, not just mathematics.

Once all of the interviews were summarized or transcribed, we analyzed them qualitatively, examining the various factors described above and attempting to discover other important contributors to learning difficulties. We now illustrate our findings through several case studies.

## *Jessica*

Jessica, a woman in her early thirties, was pursuing a master's degree in psychology and considering further work toward a Ph.D. in a related area. She agreed to participate in the study because she hoped to gain some insight into her problems with mathematics and, perhaps, get some tutoring in it.

***History.*** Jessica claimed that her family had never held high academic expectations for her and that throughout high school and college she did not value academic success. She disliked going to school and would often skip class. In high school her mathematics grades were very poor—mostly C's and D's. Despite all this, when she studied for the mathematics section of the SAT, she managed to do fairly well, scoring 600. We can attribute her success partly to some basic mathematics competence that allowed her to learn a good deal of material in a short period of time.

In college, she was more interested in socializing than study. During those "hippie days," as she put it, few people were career oriented, and she lacked the motivation to get good grades. Further, she took no mathematics or science classes in college or since, so that her familiarity with mathematics was limited to what she learned in high school.

Although academic achievement was not important for Jessica in high school and college, the situation had changed by the time we interviewed her. She enjoyed classes in graduate school and was doing fairly well in them. She maintained that she now had relatively high standards of achievement. Part of her new-found academic interest had to do with the fact that she was dissatisfied with her job and was looking for a new career.

When we saw her, Jessica was faced with the specific task of getting a good score on the quantitative section of the GRE so that she could obtain admission to a Ph.D. program. But scoring high would be difficult, because she had been avoiding mathematics for years. As Jessica put it, "I'm realizing that I really don't do a lot of things that have to do with numbers, and I really don't have a problem with arithmetic, but I guess I just don't like to do these things."

*Motivation.* Jessica felt that her problem was primarily motivational; in fact, she "hated" mathematics. "I didn't have much motivation to do well in math aside from that I didn't want to do too poorly," she remarked. Demonstrating what Dweck would describe as a performance orientation, Jessica was particularly concerned with her standing relative to that of others. This became evident when she reviewed sample problems from the Graduate Record Examination (GRE). The GRE practice test booklet consists of problems taken from past exams, along with the answers to the problems, and for each problem the percentage of previous examinees who obtained the correct answer. Jessica paid close attention to these percentages. For example, after solving a problem correctly, Jessica immediately looked up the percentage of correct responses and exclaimed, "I'm glad I got it right since 91 percent of the people who took this test did." When Jessica had difficulty with a problem solved correctly by a relatively small percentage, she did not feel bad, "because they [those who answered correctly] were probably all engineering students." However, she was disturbed that she got some problems wrong that others found easy and was surprised that she got one answer right that others found hard. Further, information concerning others' performance also influenced which problems she concentrated on and subsequently learned. When she noted that only a small percentage of the population answered a problem correctly, she gave up on it. However, if more than 50 percent of the population could solve the problem, then she might invest energy in understanding it.

Jessica's concern with social comparison also revealed itself on the projective test. When looking at a picture of a girl working on some mathematics problems in a classroom filled with other students, Jessica described her as "pretty anxious. . . . She's trying to think of something, and she doesn't look like she's daydreaming. . . . She looks a little worried and she's wondering if she's the only one in the class who's having this much difficulty. She may be looking up to see how other students are reacting."

As we have seen, Jessica's primary aim was to avoid "doing too poorly," especially in comparison with others, and she had little interest in the material itself. This performance orientation seemed to result in massive avoidance of mathematics and lack of effort. For example, Jessica spent very little time studying for the quantitative section of the GRE, although she invested considerable effort in working on the verbal section, an area in which she anticipated a high score. In fact, every time she came to the sessions, she mentioned she did not have time to work on the mathematics problems, although she was able to work on the other sections.

Jessica's lack of effort also interfered with the memorization of specific formulas. Although she had repeatedly encountered the formula for the circumference of a circle and could use it successfully, she never bothered to memorize it. In fact, she confessed later that she missed a GRE problem because of this.

***Beliefs.*** Jessica held contradictory views of mathematics. On the one hand, she believed that mathematics involves "some inner conceptualization, abstract thinking and reasoning, or logic." On the other hand, most of her work was governed by the belief that "mathematics really involves the manipulation of numbers in a sophisticated and complicated way." (Simple arithmetic and measuring, activities she could do well, were not considered mathematics. In this sense, she did not give herself credit for the mathematical skills that she did have.) Success in mathematics, she felt, involves knowing what algorithms to apply to particular problems.

This naive faith in algorithms clearly affected her work. She would often write down algorithms and occasionally try to memorize them (although not very diligently) rather than attempt to understand the logic behind their use. When she did not know the "convoluted formula" to a problem, she would often give up before even attempting a solution. When told that a problem could be solved by commonsense reasoning or by some unorthodox method, she refused to learn the alternative method, because she believed the key to solving the problem was only in the formula. She remarked, "I'm sure if you just knew some formula you would be able to figure it out," but then added reluctantly, "on the other hand, I guess there may be some other way."

***Cognition and Style.*** Jessica managed to function well in graduate school, was reasonably articulate, had serious interests, and generally appeared to be an intelligent person. It is hard to believe that her difficulties in mathematics stemmed from general deficiencies in cognitive function. Rather, her poor achievement seemed to involve two other cognitive components. One was simply lack of knowledge and familiarity with the material. Jessica last studied mathematics in high school and had avoided it since then. She had clearly forgotten some relevant terms, definitions, formulas, and the like. Given the proper motivation—which Jessica did not have—an intelligent person could reacquire this kind of knowledge fairly quickly.

A second, and more important, component contributing to Jessica's problem was her passivity. Thus, in class, she always felt as though she understood the material presented, but was surprised that she became confused once she was required "to put the pieces together for myself." Perhaps the reason for the apparent clarity at the outset is that she passively accepted the material being presented, attempting mainly to memorize the formulas but not investing the energy in learning the ideas behind the rules.

She also demonstrated a rigid cognitive style that sometimes manifested itself in resistance to learning new methods of solving problems. For example, given the problem of determining whether 1/6 or 16 percent is larger, she converted both terms into fractions with denominator 100. Then, knowing that 16 percent is 16/100, she converted it into 8/50 and 4/25. She next converted 1/6 into 4/24 and was thus able to correctly solve the problem by comparing 4/25 and 4/24. However, when it was pointed out to her that her cumbersome method might give difficulty if she was working with more complicated fractions and that she could have saved time simply by converting 1/6 into a percentage, she rigidly adhered to the idea that her method was better. Although it was repeatedly demonstrated to her that decimals, fractions, ratios, and percentages were all different ways of representing similar relationships, she never quite believed this. At one point she said, "I see how it works, but I don't really understand why it works." Yet, Jessica never attempted to understand how these concepts were related by working through the problems on her own. In brief, Jessica's passivity and rigidity have prevented her from acquiring better math skills and indeed have the effect of preserving her lack of familiarity with the subject.

*Affect.* It was obvious throughout the sessions that Jessica disliked mathematics, and she unabashedly remarked on several occasions that she "hated it." In fact, she gave the impression that life would be better if mathematics did not exist, and she resented the necessity to involve herself with it to score well on the GRE.

Part of Jessica's hatred for mathematics had to do with the fact that it made her anxious in testing situations, although not when she worked alone. She admitted to having a certain degree of test anxiety in general but felt this was amplified for mathematics tests because her ability was poor. Also, her confidence in her ability to do mathematics was low, although this was not the case in other areas of her life.

Jessica acknowledged that her lack of confidence, anxiety, and ability were interrelated. She described her problem in mathematics as stemming from a poor background, which resulted in test anxiety, as well as anxious feelings connected with wanting to do well. In turn, these feelings of anxiety contributed to her dislike and avoidance of mathematics. The anxiety appears to reproduce itself, for it interferes with the very activity (the acquisition of better skills) that would help reduce it.

***Identity.*** Aside from wanting to do well on the GRE, Jessica did not appear to care that she did poorly in mathematics. Rather, she had little use for it. "It's really too late for me to get involved with it," she remarked, "I just don't concern myself with it." Her lack of interest in mathematics did not seem to be motivated by a sex role stereotype to the effect that women should not do well in mathematics. There was no mention of the belief that mathematics is a primarily male field or that men are prejudiced against women who do well in mathematics.

Instead, Jessica seemed to identify strongly with the humanities and not the sciences. At one point, she expressed irritation that the reading comprehension questions on the GRE were all science oriented; she felt this was unfair, as she had little familiarity with science topics. "Science is one subject I just don't read much about." She prided herself on being skilled in verbal areas. She had worked as a journalist, and believed that writing was one of her strengths. Her hobbies included ballet and crossword puzzles, and she had a variety of political interests.

Jessica's lack of success in mathematics did not threaten her basic identity but bothered her only to the extent that she felt she needed to do well on the GRE. Since her identity did not include involvement in mathematics, she felt a relatively small need to shift her interests or improve her skills. In fact, in some respects, she seemed to derive some comfort from her math anxiety, since it provided a convenient excuse for not taking the time to learn mathematics.

***Conclusions.*** First, the case of Jessica reinforces our basic point that intellectual performance is affected by far more than cognitive factors alone. Jessica was typical of most successful graduate students in at least two respects: her basic cognitive abilities were quite adequate, and she was clever enough to make it through standard mathematics examinations when she had to. The cognitive factors depressing her mathematics achievement did not seem to involve basic reasoning abilities and the like but rather a lack of knowledge resulting from inexperience, a passive and rigid cognitive style, and narrow beliefs about the nature of mathematics. Furthermore, motivational and affective factors—Jessica's performance orientation, her avoidance, and her anxiety—were crucial contributors to her poor achievement.

Second, the various factors we have described interact in complex ways. Jessica employed a performance orientation that involved frequent social comparison and seemed to lead eventually to avoidance and lack of effort. This in turn hurt her study habits and prevented her from learning. Her belief in the computational nature of mathematics fits neatly with her passivity and rigidity, and these styles in turn are consonant with her lack of effort as well as with her performance orientation.

Third, the direction of causality is muddled. Her rigidity prevents her from learning, but her failure to learn also contributes to the rigidity. Thus, if she focuses on the magic of formulas she gains no insight into underlying structure, but if she does not appreciate the structure, she has no alternative to the magic formula. Similarly, her anxiety causes her to avoid mathematics, but her avoidance of it prevents her from learning, which in turn increases her anxiety. A simple notion of causality does not seem useful in explaining complexities like these.

Fourth, the cognitive and affective stand in at least two relations with each other. On the one hand, affect seems to influence effort and cognition (which in turn influence affect), as when Jessica's anxiety seems to cause avoidance of mathematics, which results in poor opportunities for learning (which in turn causes more anxiety). On the other hand, affect seems to be a part of intellectual activity. When Jessica was in an evaluation situation, anxiety was part of her mathematical work, just as much as her operations on the numbers.

Fifth, all the factors considered—affect, motivation, beliefs, style—must be interpreted within the context of Jessica's identity. Since Jessica's identity revolved around the humanities, the lack of success in mathematics, the weak effort, the narrow view of the subject, the passive and rigid style, and the unpleasant affect were not debilitating to the sense of self. Rather, they were side issues, perhaps minor obstacles on a road leading in another direction entirely. Of course, if these obstacles did not exist, perhaps another direction would have been taken in the first place; here, too, causality is muddled.

Sixth, the explanations in terms of motivation, style, affect, and belief are valuable but somewhat unsatisfying since they are silent with respect to origins and dynamics. Explanations such as these are superficial in the sense that they deal with what is on the surface. We see that the performance orientation clearly influences Jessica's behavior. But we go further and ask why she developed such an orientation and why she maintains it. What are the origins of the rigidity, of the sense of identity? Why does this complex system operate as it does? Answering questions such as these requires a dynamic and developmental psychology. The cases of Lucy and some others help us deal with some of these issues.

## *Lucy (and Some Others)*

The phenomena involving affect, belief, motivation, and cognition already observed in Jessica are by no means atypical. Lucy exhibits many of the same characteristics, as do some of our other subjects.

*Affect.* A rather dramatic woman of about 50, Lucy claimed that she "almost fainted, almost died" when she had to deal with mathematics and became "nauseous, tense, with a buzzing in my ears." At one point, during a problem-solving session, she insisted in terminating her work lest she throw up in the office, a possibility neither she nor the investigator wished to explore. Clearly for Lucy, emotion was a part—a very unpleasant part—of her intellectual work in this area, and her mathematical thinking did not operate in some emotional void. Emotion and cognition were blended in an ongoing activity. Cognition is "cold" and affectless mainly when we abstract it from the living reality.

*Motivation.* Lucy's anxiety was so intense that it also motivated her to avoid mathematics at all costs, not studying until she thought it absolutely necessary to do so. Then, when finally engaged in mathematical work, she typically took a brief, superficial look at a problem, ignoring many important details. She often came to a solution quickly, without a careful thought, and did not check her work. Perhaps both the procrastination and the impulsivity serve the function of avoiding serious engagement with the anxiety-provoking task.

*Belief.* Further, Lucy maintained the explicit belief that mathematics must be done quickly. "I want to get it done fast, and I don't like to show the guts of it, the messiness of the page. I don't want to work through it. I want to have the answer come from the sky. Everyone else gets it quickly." Lucy's theory of mathematics learning is widely shared. Many students (and teachers and parents) believe that mathematics is a subject in which one attempts to get right answers as quickly as possible. Our subjects did not believe or understand that mathematics is a way of thinking and that it is quite normal to struggle through to a solution that may be only one of several possible. It is an incredible commentary on our educational system that otherwise intelligent adults should hold such a distorted view of a fundamental feature of our culture.

*Style and Cognition.* Lucy's mathematical work exhibited a schizophrenic quality. Her rigid use of procedures—when in doubt, do something—prevented her from employing intuitions and other aspects of informal and formal knowledge in which she was not deficient. Indeed, Lucy felt that she could understand the principles underlying mathematics but had trouble with written numbers themselves. When solving a problem, Lucy operated mechanically, without understanding the reasons for a calculation. "I seem to want to get a solution and get on with it. I don't want to be bothered about all of the possibilities." Yet, when pressed, Lucy could come up with sensible explanations of what she was doing. She had available some useful formal principles and informal metaphors, but she did not ordinarily use them. Her problem was not so much a lack of skill in some area of even deficient concepts. Rather, she lacked easy connections among the different areas of her mathematical knowledge.

Several of our subjects displayed this kind of approach. For example, Allison was given a problem in which the goal was to determine whether a sum of two fractions was correct (for example, 1/32 + 3/16 = 1 1/8). She engaged in extensive calculations, converting to common denominators and getting into a good deal of trouble along the way. A simpler solution would have been to look at the relative magnitudes of the fractions, noticing that since they were both much less than a half, they could not possibly add up to a sum larger than one. But Allison, like others, failed to connect the formula with her common sense.

As we have seen, this situation is not at all uncommon. Many children, and at least some adults too, see mathematics as a disembodied computational activity unrelated to either the external or personal worlds. The lack of connections prevents them from understanding what they are doing and from correctly applying their available skills.

*Development and Identity.* Why did Lucy develop the patterns observed? Perhaps the story originates in Lucy's early relation with her mother (for much of her life, the father was not present). Lucy desperately wanted her mother's approval. She was "beguiled" by her mother and her views: "Whatever she said, went." She tried to be a "good girl," to live up to the maternal expectations, because her father had left home earlier and "I didn't want to lose this one too." She would sell herself short rather than oppose her mother, even when she belittled much of what Lucy did. Her mother felt Lucy was a poor learner and that to get her to learn she needed to "open up her head and pour the information in." The mother had difficulty with mathematics and conveyed her dislike of the subject. It was acceptable for girls to develop at least minimal skills in reading, but mathematics was another matter. Further, Lucy's mother had little interest in intellectual matters generally and seldom discussed school topics. "But we never connected." Lucy got very little help with homework. If her mother had planned some activity, it would take precedence over the homework, which would be put off or would not get done altogether.

Sometime during the elementary school years, Lucy developed a passion for the arts. At first, she exhibited an interest in sewing and later in drama and painting. Most important, Lucy saw these passions as her own property—"Sewing was mine"—that her mother could do nothing to interfere with it. Her mother was skeptical about her interests in the arts, paid little attention to them, and did not encourage them, even in later years when Lucy wanted to make a career in the area.

For Lucy, then, school learning, and mathematics in particular, were areas in which she was not expected to perform competently. At one level, she was so desperate to get her mother's approval that she molded her self-concept to fit the expectation and indeed became a poor learner. At another level, she carved out for herself an identity with which her mother could not interfere—an identity connected with the arts, not with conventional schooling. She was willing to be dumb in school to conform with her mother's image but saved for herself a passion for the arts.

No doubt this story, as told by Lucy, is incomplete and partly inaccurate. For one thing, it does not seem to explain the remarkable intensity of Lucy's dread of mathematics, extending even to nausea. Despite this, the story makes clear that Lucy's intellectual difficulties must be considered from a developmental point of view, in the context of her relation with her mother and her identity.

## *Woody and Mary*

We propose that it is generally true that intellect must be considered within the context of personality. Consider the examples provided by two undergraduates. Woody was a college student experiencing considerable difficulty in his studies. He came from a family in which his father was a professor of mathematics and his older brother was an excellent student in chemistry and computers. Woody felt strong pressure to excel in academic work and to go on to a career in mathematics, as had his father and brother. Woody gave the impression of being effeminate. When he realized that the interview was to be videotaped, he said, in a half-joking fashion, "If we're going to be on camera, I'll fix my hair." He consistently used fancified language, referring, for example, to a picture of a brutish-looking person as "this gentleman" and describing his own depression as "early morning awakening psychomotor retardation." In response to one of the pictures of the projective test—a person sitting with some books in a cozy living room—he said: "This young man is studying organic chemistry and is in a very comfortable home, and he's not too pleased studying because he sort of feels like he'd really rather be over here eating this banana. . . . There's attractive fruit over here. He eats the fruit and smells the flowers, and you really wonder why he's taking such hard science courses." Like the young man in his story, Woody felt that he must take hard science courses because that is the masculine thing to do, as determined by his father and brother's example. But at a deeper level, Woody's preferred identity was feminine. He would rather smell the flowers. Our interpretation is that Woody's academic difficulties were related to his identity conflict. He needed to find what he defines as a feminine outlet for his intellectual concerns.

For students struggling with issues like these, intellectual growth often involves finding a way to connect significant personal concerns with school learning. Mary, an undergraduate, shied away from mathematics and instead developed an interest in understanding and helping others. "One of the reasons that I'm interested in counseling is that . . . I grew up in an alcoholic home. It was extremely difficult. It has determined a lot of my interests in the ways in which I want to help people, and also I'm fascinated by alcoholics. I'm also interested in literature because I feel there are certain authors who write about how individuals come to feel certain ways and make certain choices and by studying that it makes more clear my own recent behavior. . . . Having had painful experiences growing up with my mother's alcoholism, I am able to have compassion with other people's pain, and I am naturally drawn to helping people to try to learn certain things about themselves."

Sometimes Mary can muster little enthusiasm for school work. She finds it hard to concentrate on her studies and does slipshod work. Why? Mary feels that many of her difficulties in academic work stem from its isolation from her personal concerns. "Academic life is definitely separate from your personal life, separate from your family life . . . but you can't separate it entirely . . . and when you ignore that, a lot of problems come up. . . . Academics is a very personal thing. . . . It is based not only on intellectual things but on emotional things." As her confused presentation indicates, Mary is obviously struggling with these issues. For her, the central learning problem is to find a way to relate her studies to the meaningful issues of her life. If this cannot be done, she suffers from lack of interest and motivation.

## Conclusions

Our exploratory research points to a few general conclusions. One is that, at least in the case of individuals suffering from learning difficulties, mathematical thinking is clearly "hot": it is bound up with emotions, beliefs, styles, motives, and identity. We use the ambiguous phrase "bound up with" because the relations among these factors or processes and mathematical thinking are complex. In one sense, some of the factors are parts of mathematical thinking in the real world. Mathematical thinking is more than strategies and concepts. It is also, for example, fearful, dependent, and persistent. We might even say that thinking has a "personality" that needs to be described and explained.

In this view, we need to broaden our conception of what mathematical thinking and thinking in general is all about. Mathematical thinking is more than strategies, knowledge, and procedures. Contrary to Piaget, intellectual activity is not primarily the operation of logico-mathematical structures motivated by natural curiosity. Contrary to the information-processing theorists, intellectual activity is not primarily the operation of procedural and declarative knowledge. Instead, at least in those suffering from learning difficulties—and who does not in some degree?—mathematical thinking is in significant measure the operation of beliefs, feelings, motives, and the like. As Dewey (1933) pointed out many years ago, intellectual activity does not exist in isolation from other aspects of the person. And we suspect that this proposition holds true not only for those with serious learning problems but for all of us.

A second sense of "bound up with" is that mathematical thinking is influenced by the various factors in complex ways. Clearly, mathematical performance is not determined by intelligence or mathematical ability alone. The students whom we investigated did not seem to suffer from basic intellectual deficiencies that could explain their learning problems. Instead, their intellectual performance was influenced by a number of strictly noncognitive factors. Anxiety depresses performance; rigidity prevents learning; beliefs inhibit exploration and hence learning. At the same time, the direction of causality is not always clear: thus anxiety promotes avoidance, but avoidance produces poor performance, which in turn promotes anxiety. In brief, mathematical performance is composed of noncognitive factors, is influenced by them, and influences them.

Second, to understand the complex nature of hot cognition, or the personality of cognition, we need to consider both dynamics and development. With respect to the former, we have seen that the processes described "interact" in complex ways. Thus, ability influences style (you cannot be resourceful unless you have intellectual resources to deploy); belief affects strategy (if you think mathematics involves quick, correct answers, you are not likely to make sense of the material); an identity determines motivation (if you see yourself as an arts person, you may avoid mathematics). We propose that understanding these kinds of interactions among cognitive and noncognitive factors requires a dynamic theory—a theory describing how the various factors operate as a system. Thus, we need to understand how the observed cognitive activity, style, feeling, and motivation operate within the context of the individual's identity and general personality structure.

Developing such a theory is an important task for the future. We suspect that one important resource for such a theory is the "ego psychology" stemming from the psychoanalytic tradition, as exemplified by the work of such writers as Shapiro (1965). In this tradition, cognitive functioning, in both the "normal" and pathological sense, is seen as but one aspect of ego development, which in turn must be understood in the context of the dynamics of personality, including such matters as the ways in which cognitive styles emerge from the functioning of defense mechanisms. In other words, the personality of cognition must be understood in terms of the dynamics of personality.

It must also be understood in the context of development. Hot cognition has a history, and this history may often involve relations with parents or significant others. Understanding of thinking-emotion-motivation requires a truly developmental approach that attempts to elucidate the meaning of current styles, emotions, and motives in terms of attempts to cope with early experiences of various types. Thus, a performance orientation may be understood by reference to a dependency relation with a parent; an a-historical approach sheds little light on the developmental meaning of the motivation.

We believe further that theorizing concerning both dynamics and development can profitably stem from detailed case studies of the sort we have presented here. The standard laboratory test and observational techniques of developmental psychology are inherently inadequate to the task of capturing the development of complex dynamic relations.

Finally, our approach to understanding learning difficulties in the context of personality suggests a somewhat different approach to education. In our view, education is more than acquiring information or cognitive skills or getting good grades on tests. For many students, education is not only the cognitive activity we thought it was, it is something more personal, more deep. Most crucially, it involves finding personal meaning in what is taught in school. One critical aspect of education involves the integration of the formal into the personal. This in turn is intimately bound up with the development of identity, or defense mechanisms, of emotional attachments. Real learning is not just mastering skills; it is at least, in part, the process of creating meaning by connecting what is taught to what is important to the individual.

One way of interpreting this kind of integration is in terms of Piaget's and Vygotsky's theories. Piaget ([1936] 1952) pointed out that assimilation is the "prime fact of mental life." By this he meant that we always interpret the new data of experience in terms of what we already know—that is, in terms of existing structures. For many students, the new data are the subjects taught in school, and the most important existing structures are their personal identities. (Thus Mary had to integrate schoolwork with her concern with understanding and relating to others.) Vygotsky (1962) pointed out that the chief task for education is to integrate spontaneous and schooled knowledge, to blend the personal and the social. For many students, the integration must involve not only schooled knowledge with informal knowledge (for example, written and mental arithmetic), but it must also involve connecting schooled knowledge with intimate personal concerns. If that kind of integration is not achieved, then for many individuals schooling, however successful it may appear to be by conventional criteria, is merely "academic"—that is, it is unimportant, personally meaningless, and irrelevant. Is it not a crime that for many of our students, academic knowledge is seen as cold and irrelevant to their personal lives, that it has not been assimilated in any meaningful way?

The study of hot cognition thus points the way to more meaningful education. If knowledge is also emotion and motive, and if knowledge develops in the context of the dynamic personality, then education must involve more than the transmission and even reinvention of knowledge.

## References

Allardice, B. S., and Ginsburg, H. P. "Children's Psychological Difficulties in Mathematics." In H. P. Ginsburg (ed.), *The Development of Mathematical Thinking.* Orlando, Fla.: Academic Press, 1983.

Bandura, A. "Self-referent Thought: A Developmental Analysis of Self-efficacy." In J. H. Flavell and L. Ross (eds.), *Social Cognitive Development.* New York: Cambridge University Press, 1981.

Baroody, A. J., Ginsburg, H. P., and Waxman, B. "Children's Use of Mathematical Structure." *Journal for Research in Mathematics Education,* 1983, *14,* 156-168.

Benbow, C. P., and Stanley, J. C. "Intellectually Talented Boys and Girls: Educational Profiles." *Gifted Child Quarterly,* 1982, *24,* 82-88.

Brown, A., Bransford, J. D., Ferrara, R. A., and Campione, J. C. "Learning, Remembering, and Understanding." In P. Mussen (ed.), *Handbook of Child Psychology.* Vol. 3: *Cognitive Development.* New York: Wiley, 1983.

Brush, L. R. "A Validation Study of the Mathematics Anxiety Rating Scale (MARS)." *Educational and Psychological Measurement,* 1978, *38,* 485-490.

Brush, L. R. "Some Thoughts for Teachers on Mathematics Anxiety." *Arithmetic Teacher,* 1981, *29,* 37-39.

Carraher, T. N., Carraher, D. W., and Schliemann, A. S. "Mathematics in the Streets and in Schools." *British Journal of Developmental Psychology,* 1985, *3,* 21-29.

Dewey, J. *How We Think.* Chicago: Gateway, 1933.

Donaldson, M. *Children's Minds.* New York: Norton, 1978.

Dweck, C. S., Davidson, W., Nelson, S., and Enna, B. "Sex Differences in Learned Helplessness: II. The Contingencies of Evaluative Feedback in the Classroom; III. An Experimental Analysis." *Developmental Psychology,* 1978, *14,* 268-276.

Dweck, C. S., and Elliot, E. S. "Achievement Motivation." In P. Mussen (gen. ed.) and E. M. Hetherington (vol. ed.), *Handbook of Child Psychology.* Vol. 4. New York: Wiley, 1983.

Entwistle, D. R., and Hayduk, L. A. *Too Great Expectations: The Academic Outlook of Young Children.* Baltimore, Md.: Johns Hopkins University Press, 1978.

Ernest, J. "Mathematics and Sex." *American Mathematical Monthly,* 1976, *82,* 595-612.

Ginsburg, H. P. *Children's Arithmetic: How They Learn It and How You Teach It.* (2nd ed.) Austin, Tex.: Pro Ed, in press.

Ginsburg, H. P., Posner, J. K., and Russell, R. L. "The Development of Mental Addition as a Function of Schooling and Culture." *Journal of Cross-Cultural Psychology,* 1981, *12,* 163-176.

Ginsburg, H. P., and Russell, R. L. "Social Class and Racial Influences on Early Mathematical Thinking." *Monographs of the Society for Research in Child Development,* 1981, *46* (6), serial no. 193.

McCloskey, M., and Caramazza, A. "Cognitive Mechanisms in Number Processing and Calculation: Evidence from Dyscalculia." *Brain and Cognition,* 1985, *4,* 171-196.

McKnight, C. C., Crosswhite, F. J., Dossey, J. A., Kifer, E., Swafford, J. O., Travers, K. J., and Cooney, T. J. *The Underachieving Curriculum: Assessing U.S. School Mathematics from an International Perspective.* Champaign, Ill.: Stipes, 1987.

Messick, S. "The Nature of Cognitive Styles: Problems and Promise in Educational Practice." *Educational Psychologist,* 1984, *19,* 59-74.

Mueller, E. C., and Ginsburg, H. P. "The MUG Projective Test," forthcoming.

Parsons, J. E., Adler, T. F., and Kaczala, C. "Socialization of Achievement Attitudes and Beliefs: Parental Influences." *Child Development*, 1982, *53*, 310-321.
Piaget, J. *The Origins of Intelligence in Children*. New York: International Universities Press, 1952. (Originally published 1936.)
Piaget, J. *The Science of Education and the Psychology of the Child*. New York: Orion Press, 1970. (Originally published 1935.)
Reyes, L. H. "Affective Variables and Mathematics Education." *The Elementary School Journal*, 1984, *84*, 558-580.
Richardson, F. C., and Suinn, R. M. "The Mathematics Anxiety Rating Scale: Psychometric Data." *Journal of Counseling Psychology*, 1972, *19*, 551-554.
Saxe, G., and Posner, J. K. "The Development of Numerical Cognition: Cross-Cultural Perspectives." In H. P. Ginsburg (ed.), *The Development of Mathematical Thinking*. Orlando, Fla.: Academic Press, 1983.
Scribner, S. "Pricing Delivery Tickets: 'School Arithmetic' in a Practical Setting." *The Quarterly Newsletter of the Laboratory of Comparative Human Cognition*, 1984, *6*, 19-25.
Shapiro, D. *Neurotic Styles*. New York: Basic Books, 1965.
Sherman, J. "Mathematics, Spatial Visualization and Related Factors: Changes in Girls and Boys, Grades 8-11." *Journal of Educational Psychology*, 1980, *72*, 476-482.
Shiffler, N., Lynch-Sauer, J., and Nadelman, L. "Relationship Between Self-concept and Classroom Behavior in Two Informal Elementary Classrooms." *Journal of Educational Psychology*, 1977, *69*, 349-359.
Stein, A. "The Effects of Sex-Role Standards for Achievement and Sex-Role Preference on Three Determinants of Achievement Motivation." *Developmental Psychology*, 1971, *4*, 219-231.
Stevenson, H. W., Stigler, J. S., Lee, S., Lucker, G. W., Kitamura, S., and Hsu, C. "Cognitive Performance and Academic Achievement of Japanese, Chinese, and American Children." *Child Development*, 1985, *56*, 718-734.
Stigler, J. W., and Perry, M. "Cross-Cultural Studies of Mathematics Teaching and Learning: Recent Findings and New Directions." Paper delivered at the NSF-NCTM Research Agenda Conference, Columbia, Mo., March 1987.
Stodolsky, S. S. "Telling Math: Origins of Math Aversion and Anxiety." *Educational Psychologist*, 1985, *20*, 125-133.
Tobias, S., and Weissbrod, C. "Anxiety and Mathematics: An Update." *Harvard Educational Review*, 1980, *50*, 63-70.
Vygotsky, L. S. *Thought and Language*. Cambridge, Mass.: MIT Press, 1962.

*Herbert P. Ginsburg is professor of psychology and education at Teachers College, Columbia University.*

*Kirsten A. Asmussen is a graduate student and instructor at Teachers College, Columbia University.*

# *Index*

## A

Abacus: adaptive expertise with, 62-65; and street math, 2, 65-66
Adaptive expertise, 68-69; with abacus, 62-65; instructional implications of, 66-68; model of, 57-62; and routine expertise, 55-57; of street math, 65-66
Adler, T. F., 96, 111
Affect, and math learning difficulties, 95
Allardice, B. S., 79, 86, 90, 110
Allport, D. A., 9, 23
Amaiwa, S., 64, 69
American classrooms, 51-53; coherence in, 46-51; evaluation in, 43-46; math knowledge in, 30-32; observation methods in, 32-35; organization in, 35-39; problem solving in, 39-43
American students, math achievement of, 28
Antell, S. R., 21, 23
Arithmetic cognition, 1, 5-6, 23; components of, 9-20; and culture, 20-23; model of, 6-9
Arithmetic operations, oral versus written, 74-79
Ashton, P., 21, 22, 23
Asian students, math achievement of, 28
Asmussen, K. A., 2, 89, 111

## B

Bandura, A., 95, 110
Baroody, A. J., 22, 25, 93, 110
Beliefs, and math learning difficulties, 93
Benbow, C. P., 96, 110
Berliner, D. C., 49, 53
Berlyne, D. E., 58, 69
Blevins-Knabe, B., 19, 23
Bransford, J. D., 95, 110
Brazil: foremen's math in, 80-82; street math in, 2, 65-66, 74-79

Brown, A., 95, 110
Brush, L. R., 19, 23, 91, 92, 110
Bryant, P., 20, 23

## C

Campione, J. C., 95, 110
Caramazza, A., 90, 110
Carey, S., 57, 69
Carraher, D. W., 2, 65, 66, 69, 71, 72, 74, 75, 76, 77, 78, 86, 87, 91, 110
Carraher, T. N., 2, 65, 66, 69, 71, 72, 74, 75, 76, 77, 78, 79, 81, 82, 85, 86, 87, 91, 110
Chi, M.T.H., 55, 69
Chinese classrooms, 51-53; coherence in, 46-51; evaluation in, 43-46; math knowledge in, 30-32; observation method for, 32-35; organization in, 35-39; problem solving in, 39-43
Classrooms, comparative studies of, 1, 27-53. *See also* American classrooms; Chinese classrooms; Japanese classrooms
Cognitive styles, and math learning difficulties, 94-95
Coherence, in Asian and American classrooms, 46-51
Cole, M., 86
Computational procedures, 6-8, 15-18, 23; and culture, 21-22
Concepts, 72-74
Conceptual knowledge: acquisition of, 57, 68-69; of experts, 56-57; and procedural knowledge, 84-86. *See also* Adaptive expertise
Cooney, T. J., 53, 54
Cooper, R. G., 9, 19, 21, 23, 25
Correspondence construction, 6, 11-13, 14-15, 23; and computation, 16-17; and culture, 21-22
Counting, 6, 7, 13-15, 23; and computation, 17-18; and culture, 22
Cross-process sequences, 14-15, 23
Crosswhite, F. J., 53, 54

113

Culture: and arithmetic cognition, 20-23; and math ability, 51-52
Cunha, T.M.V., 79, 86
Curtis, L. E., 21, 25

### D

Dasen, P. R., 21, 22, 23, 71, 86
Davidson, W., 94, 110
de la Rocha, O., 72, 87
Dewey, J., 107, 110
Donaldson, M., 90, 110
Dossey, J. A., 53, 54
Dweck, C. S., 93-94, 96, 99, 110

### E

Elliot, E. S., 93-94, 110
Enna, B., 94, 110
Entwistle, D. R., 95, 110
Enumerative processes, 6, 7, 9-15, 23; and culture, 21-22
Ernest, J., 91, 96, 110
Evaluation: in Asian and American classrooms, 43-46, 52; and gender, 94

### F

Ferrara, R. A., 95, 110
Fishermen, math of, 82-84
Flexibility, 84
Foremen, scale knowledge of, 80-82
Frydman, O., 20, 23
Fuson, K. C., 17, 23-24

### G

Gallistel, C. R., 6, 13, 14, 19, 20, 24
Garcia, R., 72, 87
Gay, J., 86
Gearhart, M., 3, 5n, 6, 21, 25
Gelman, R., 6, 13, 14, 17, 18, 19, 20, 24, 25
Gender: and expectations, 96; and feedback, 94
Gentner, D., 56, 69
Ginsburg, H. P., 2, 6, 20, 21, 22, 24, 25, 79, 86, 89, 90, 91, 93, 97, 110, 111
Glaser, R., 55, 69
Glick, J., 86

Gréco, P., 20, 24
Greene, D., 59, 70
Greeno, J. G., 14, 24, 47, 53, 56, 69
Groen, G. J., 18, 24
Guberman, S. R., 6, 21, 25

### H

Hall, J. W., 17, 23-24
Hart, K., 79, 86
Hatano, G., 2, 55, 56, 57, 58, 63, 64, 66-67, 68, 69, 70, 78, 80, 87
Hayduk, L. A., 95, 110
Hiebert, J., 56, 69-70
Horizontal decalage, 72
"Hot mathematics," 2, 89, 107-109
Hsu, C., 27n
Husen, T., 28, 53
Hypothesis-Experiment-Instruction, 67-68

### I

Identity, and math learning difficulties, 95-96
Inagaki, K., 56, 57, 58, 59, 61, 62, 67, 68, 69, 70
Inhelder, B., 20, 24
Itakura, K., 67, 70

### J

Japan: abacus in, 2, 62-66; science in, 67-68. See also Asian students
Japanese classrooms, 51-53; coherence in, 46-51; evaluation in, 43-46; math knowledge in, 30-32; math lesson in, 28-29; observation method for, 32-35; organization in, 35-39; problem solving in, 39-43
Johnson, D. W., 62, 70
Johnson, R. T., 62, 70

### K

Kaczala, C., 96, 111
Kato, T., 27n
Keating, D., 21, 23
Kifer, E., 53
Kimura, S., 27n
Kitamura, S., 27n
Klahr, D., 9, 10, 24

Klein, A., 1, 5, 16, 19, 20, 21, 24, 26
Knopp, K., 19, 24
Knowledge. *See* Conceptual knowledge; Mathematical knowledge; Procedural knowledge

**L**

Lancy, D. F., 22, 24
Langer, J., 11, 19, 21, 24
Language arts, 35-36
Lave, J., 72, 87
Lee, S. Y., 27n, 28, 32, 37, 38, 39, 51, 53
Lefevre, P., 56, 69-70
Leinhardt, G., 47, 53
Leitner, E., 23
Lepper, M. R., 59, 70
Lézine, I., 25
Lucker, G. W., 32, 53
Lynch-Sauer, J., 95, 111

**M**

McCloskey, M., 90, 110
Mace, P. G., 23
McKnight, C. C., 28, 53, 54, 90, 110
Mandler, G., 9, 24
Manipulatives, 40-43
Mao, L., 27n
Markman, E. M., 60, 70
Math anxiety, 90
Math Anxiety Rating Scale, 97
Mathematical concepts, 71-74, 84-86
Mathematical knowledge, American versus Asian, 30-32
Mathematics: oral versus written, 74-79; street, 2, 65-66
Mathematics achievement, American versus Asian, 28
Mathematics learning difficulties, 89-90; case examples of, 98-107; conclusions on, 107-109; instructional causes of, 92; method of study of, 97-98; noncognitive explanations for, 92-97; paradox of, 90-92
Meck, E., 14, 24
Menninger, K., 9, 21, 24
Merkin, S., 14, 24
Messick, S., 94, 111
Miranda, E. M., 79, 87
Miyake, N., 60-61, 70

Motivation, and math learning difficulties, 93-94
Motoyoshi, M., 57, 70
Mueller, E. C., 97, 111
Murtaugh, M., 72, 87

**N**

Nadelman, L., 95, 111
Nelson, S., 94, 110
New Guinea, 22, 85
Number system, 6, 8-9, 18-20, 23; and culture, 20-21

**O**

Oral mathematics, and written math, 74-79
Organization, of classroom, 36-39, 51

**P**

Parsons, J. E., 96, 111
Performance, 40
Perret-Clermont, A. N., 62, 70
Perry, M., 1, 27, 54, 92, 111
Pettito, A. L., 20, 25
Piaget, J., 6, 12-13, 16, 19, 20, 22, 24, 25, 72, 87, 90, 107, 109, 111
Policastro, M., 46, 53
Posner, J. K., 9, 21, 22, 25, 91, 110, 111
Praise, in American and Asian classrooms, 44-46, 52
Problem solving: adaptive and routine, 55-57; in Asian and American classrooms, 39-43; oral versus written, 74-79. *See also* Adaptive expertise
Procedural knowledge, and conceptual knowledge, 84-86
Proportion: fishermen's knowledge of, 82-84; worker knowledge of, 79-82

**R**

Rayna, S., 25
Reading, 35-36
Real-world scenarios, 40-43, 52
Rees, E., 55, 69
Reflection, 40, 52
Resnick, L. B., 18, 24, 77, 79, 87

Reyes, L. H., 95, 96, 111
Richardson, F. C., 97, 111
Riley, M. S., 14, 24
Robinson, M., 6, 17, 18, 25
Routine expertise, and adaptive expertise, 55-57
Russell, R. L., 6, 20, 21, 22, 24, 91, 110

**S**

Saxe, G. B., 3, 5n, 6, 9, 13, 14, 21, 22, 25, 85, 87, 91, 111
Schliemann, A. D., 2, 65, 66, 69, 71, 72, 74, 75, 76, 77, 78, 79, 85, 86, 87, 91, 110
School. See Classrooms; Written mathematics
Scribner, S., 95, 111
Self-esteem, 29
Shapiro, D., 108, 111
Sharp, D., 86
Shebo, B. J., 9, 24
Sherman, J., 96, 111
Shiffler, N., 95, 111
Siegler, R. S., 6, 17, 18, 25
Sinclair, H., 21, 25
Situations, 73-74
Smith, K., 62, 70
Song, M., 22, 25
Spiro, M. E., 29, 53
Stambak, M., 25
Stanley, J. C., 96, 110
Starkey, P., 1, 5, 9, 10, 15, 17, 18, 21, 23, 25, 26
Stein, A., 96, 111
Stein, N. L., 46, 53
Stevens, A. L., 56, 69
Stevenson, H. W., 27n, 28, 32, 37, 38, 39, 51, 53, 90, 111
Stigler, J. W., 1, 27, 27n, 28, 32, 37, 38, 39, 51, 53, 54, 92, 111
Stodolsky, S. S., 92, 111
Strauss, M. S., 21, 25

Street mathematics, 2, 65-66. See also Oral mathematics
Subitizing, 6, 9-11, 14-15, 23; and computation, 15-16; and culture, 21
Subrenat, A., 89n
Sugarman, S., 11, 12, 25
Suinn, R. M., 97, 111
Swafford, J. O., 53, 54

**T**

Tikunoff, W. J., 49, 53
Time, classroom use of, 35-36, 51
Tobias, S., 96, 111
Trabasso, T., 46, 54
Travers, K. J., 28, 53, 54
Tukey, J. W., 30, 54

**U**

Universals, in arithmetic cognition, 1, 5-6, 23

**V**

van den Broek, P., 46, 54
Verba, M., 25
Vergnaud, G., 72-74, 87
Vygotsky, L. S., 6, 25, 109, 111

**W**

Wallace, J. G., 10, 24
Waxman, B., 93, 110
Weissbrod, C., 96, 111
Wertheimer, M., 21, 26
White, M., 53, 54
Work, proportion expertise in, 79-84
Written mathematics, and oral math, 74-79

**Z**

Zaslavsky, C., 9, 22, 26

R. A. LeVine, P. M. Miller, M. M. West (eds.). *Parental Behavior in Diverse Societies.*
New Directions for Child Development, no. 40. San Francisco: Jossey-Bass, Summer 1988.

## ERRATA

Page 86, lines 4-11:

These sentences should read: In both the Gusii and Yucatec Mayan samples, mothers held their infants in virtually all their interactions with them. Other maternal behaviors, such as physical contact (apart from holding), visual regard, and verbal interaction, occurred in the context of holding. In contrast, holding occurred in only half of the U.S. mothers' interactions with their three- to four-month-olds; they often looked at and talked to their infants from a distance.